EVERLASTING WISDOM

ACHIEVE TRUE WISDOM
IN BUSINESS
BY APPLYING
TWELVE ANCIENT PRINCIPLES

by

Brian Hazelgren

Sortis Publishing

ISBN # 978-0-9772025-3-9

Printed in the United States of America

I would like to dedicate this book to my beautiful children Lindsay, BJ, Breanne, Dallin, Allison and Emily, with the hope that they will exercise wisdom in all they do in life. Not only to exercise wisdom, but to learn humility and to be teachable during this earthly journey so that they may be a shining influence in the lives of many.

Love, Dad

Table of Contents

When I was growing up my Dad used to tell me to be wise in my choices of friends, choosing my career, and how I speak to others. He would remind me that there are people who would only look out for themselves and to always make sure that I could count on my friends to do the right thing. If my friends were unwise in their choices he expected me to exercise wisdom and make the right choice.

I wish I could say that I carried out my father's request to perfection. If I had, I would not have made some of the stupid choices that I ended up making, and could have saved myself embarrassment, sleepless nights, and a little bit of sanity. Unfortunately even as an adult, I have sometimes relied on my perceived wisdom, and at times ignored the big picture.

I guess we all go through that at one point or another in our lives. You know it's when we feel like we really want to do something, and then just "know" that we ought to do x_________. "I can make this work, because, well I'm me, and I can make anything work!" Yeah, that has been me in times past…the cavalier, the maverick, the eternal optimist.

Don't get me wrong, there is nothing wrong with this confidence. I love to be around confident people, and consider myself to be one as well. I am still the optimist that believes we must follow some kind of executable plan. What I hope we can all start doing is exercising more wisdom in making decisions. My hope is that this book becomes the foundation for you to find wisdom. We can all learn from the pages penned by one of the most successful ruler's in the world's history.

My long time friend George Roumpos once told me about the "five-finger friends" in life that we should all seek to find. You can usually count on one hand how many people you can count on in life, and that these were the five-finger friends that we should never have to worry about.

Life is based on a series of choices that we make and those choices form who we are, and who we can yet become. During the course of a normal day we end up making hundreds of choices that have an effect on that particular day. Those choices can also end up charting the course set for the rest of our lives.

This book is based on a series of choices that the most successful and powerful king of his day had made, and how he eventually built a massive empire. I have become somewhat of a student of wisdom over the past few years, and the story of King Solomon is where I began my journey.

I was sitting in church one day listening to a discussion about the wisdom of King Solomon and the Proverbs that he penned. The teacher had asked a few people to come prepared to speak about a particular Proverb or Psalm. After listening to a series of two-minute overviews of their favorite passages, it struck me that those words were certainly wise 3,000 years ago, and are even more applicable to today's circumstances both personal and for business.

Then a crazy idea popped into my head…"If this wisdom is even more applicable to our day and age, then why not write a book about 'Wisdom', and make King Solomon's success the basis of the book. Then take those principles and come up with a formula of how Solomon built the most massive and powerful empire on earth."

Off I went to study up on wisdom and to become the world's foremost authority on a subject that seems to elude millions, or at least seems to be avoided by many. I can tell you that this journey is a long one, but in a short period of time, I have learned one thing…I have a long way to go to really understand how to tap into wisdom and make it work for me, my family, my business and personal relationships, and even more.

But the good news is that anyone can learn these principles and greatly enhance their personal situation…anyone.

What I have learned is that Solomon's life was made up of a pattern of choices that seemed to make his status in the community, and surrounding countries, even more advanced with each passing day.

Solomon's empire was built on choices and principles that he shares with us in several books in the Bible.

Before we go any further, please know that I consider myself to be a religious man, and I like to draw instruction and wisdom from ancient prophets and leaders. I believe that we can use their writings and advice to our benefit and build a life of principle based on solid values. I also believe that as we ponder their writings and apply good principles to our own life, that we not only help ourselves – we help others.

This book is based on the wise instruction given by Solomon, but at the very foundation is a set of 12 Key Principles that if followed will help you build a successful empire. That "empire" could be in business, in your personal life, with your career, your choice of friends, or even with your own Sunday school class!

I hope to walk you through a journey in the next few pages that will allow you to cut through the clutter and have a breakthrough moment…heck, have several breakthrough moments! I want to be your coach and help you build your future empire. *Empire Building*

101 starts here and now, and I promise you that this journey will be something that will change your thought process and ultimately change your life for the better.

Many empires have been built during the past 3,000 years since Solomon. You may even work for an empire that was started and built by someone who had vision…someone who had a little something extra in their approach to life…someone who actually felt at some point in their life that they were born to make a difference.

Although this may seem like a religious book, it was not intended to be. This book was written for the business owner; business manager; parent; or leader who has at some point realized that they want to do more in this life. Obviously *Everlasting Wisdom* is based on principles taught in the Bible, but King Solomon was not only a Biblical figure. He was the thirtieth son of Bathsheba and King David of Israel. He was born into the royal family, but did not sit back and have people build something for him. He saw opportunities for growth and development and included God in his plans.

As he amassed the largest empire in the world during his day, Solomon made his share of mistakes. The key is that he had a plan and took action; paid attention to details; sought to please God; built his empire over time…not overnight; and he held others accountable. When you study the 12 Key Principles for Building an Empire in this book, pay particular attention to each principle and how it can be used in your own life…to your own advantage.

You have at your fingertips the formula for building an empire… an empire that can be the force for doing good for you and millions of others. Enjoy the reading and by all means enjoy your journey. Since I am your coach on this empire building journey, keep me informed of your progress, and share your successes and learning experiences.

I hope to have the privilege someday of meeting you and shaking your hand, and to hear your personal story of your amazing empire-building journey.

Enter the world of Empire Building 101…CAUTION: your future empire may be just ahead, or around the corner, and I am here to prepare you to receive it. Strap in and get ready to start building!

Brian Hazelgren

CHAPTER ONE

Origins of Everlasting Wisdom:
The Timeless Wisdom of Solomon

"For as he thinketh in his heart, so is he."
-- King Solomon

What is true wisdom and who actually possesses it? Do you have it…do I? Is true wisdom something we should pursue, and if we do, how will we know when we have obtained it? It is said that *true wisdom* is something that takes years to acquire, or even a lifetime. That it is only reserved for those who have experienced many facets of life.

Definition

Wisdom, according to the Merriam-Webster dictionary, is defined as the "1 a: Accumulated philosophic or scientific learning-knowledge; b: Ability to discern inner qualities and relationships-insight; c: Good sense-judgment. 2: A wise attitude, belief, or course of action. 3: The teachings of the ancient wise men."

Wisdom is often considered to be a trait that can be developed by experience, but not necessarily taught. When applied to practical matters, the term *wisdom* is synonymous with prudence, practicality, and the tendency to avoid risk. Some see wisdom as a quality that even a child, otherwise immature, may possess independent of experience or complete knowledge. Some define wisdom in a practical sense, as foreseeing consequences and acting to maximize the long-term common good.

In general, wisdom is looked at his/her ideals and principles that govern all actions and decisions. Applications of *personal wisdom* include one's ethical and social guidelines in life that determines one's unique style of personality, the particular nature of short and long-term goal(s) pursued in life (spiritual or materialistic for example), perspective on life, social attitudes, etc.

I like to think on more simple terms however, and boil it down to making wise choices for the betterment of society or of one's soul. It's usually all of those small decisions that we make each and every day that add up to a carefully selected path.

George Washington said it succinctly: "Ninety-nine percent of the failures come from people who have the habit of making excuses."

Anne Frank, who had the wisdom of someone much older and more experienced than a teenager taught: "How wonderful it is that no one needed wait a single moment before starting to improve the world."

Confucius stated that wisdom can actually be learned by three methods: Reflection (the noblest), imitation (the easiest) and experience (the bitterest).

Buddha taught that a wise person is endowed with good bodily conduct, good verbal conduct & good mental conduct (AN3:2) and a wise person performs actions that are unpleasant to do but give good results and doesn't do actions that are pleasant to do but give bad results (AN4:115). This is called karma. The Buddha has much to say on the subject of wisdom including:

- He who arbitrates a case by force does not thereby become just. But the wise man is he who carefully discriminates between right and wrong.

- One is not wise merely because he talks much. But he who is calm, free from hatred and fear, is verily called a wise man.

- He who understands both good and evil as they really are, is called a true sage.

This book is a study about King Solomon of Israel, who was considered to be the wisest of all kings of the earth in his time. It is also a comparison of his wisdom from ancient days, and how it has transcended three millennia. He built a massive empire that was not only confined to his local region, it extended far beyond the walls of Jerusalem. His reign was 40 prosperous years, and it all started with a simple prayer where he asked God for increased wisdom to lead and bless his people.

During Solomon's long reign of 40 years, the Hebrew monarchy, according to the Bible, gained its highest splendor. This period has been called the *Augustan Age* of the Jewish annals. In a single year, according to 1 Kings 10:14, Solomon collected tribute amounting to 666 talents of gold. What we have to realize is that 666 talents equals about 600,000 troy oz., and at this writing (December 2009), gold is worth $1,165 per troy oz., would equal $699 million dollars! Even if you go back a few years to August of 1998, which at the time gold was trading at an 18 year low at $290 oz, this value was still $174 million. When you adjust for inflation, the amount is in the billions. Not a bad tribute to take in any case!

Some archaeologists consider the kingdom of Israel at the time of Solomon to have been little more than a small city state, making this an unbelievably large amount of money. What's more, the value of gold in the ancient Near East would have been far greater, as modern mining methods were not available, and they did not have access to the vast reserves that we do today.

I have been the benefactor of Solomon's wisdom by following his counsel and advice many times in my life. Yet on the other hand, I have been left to be scorned for not following prudent advice and letting my own pride get in the way. Solomon's wisdom transcends the ages, and is available to us if we will only listen to his counsel coming to us from 3,000 years ago, but it is my belief that his wisdom is even more applicable today.

Of all the qualities that Solomon possessed the one most attributed to him when you think of the stories is his wisdom. One account was of Solomon suggesting to divide a baby in two to determine its real mother, is from the Old Testament of the Bible in the book of Kings. In this often-quoted incident, two prostitutes came before Solomon to resolve a quarrel about which of them was the true mother of a baby. (The other mother's baby died in the night and each claimed the surviving child as hers.)

When Solomon suggested dividing the living child in two with a sword so both could share the baby, the true mother was revealed to him because she was willing to give up her child to the lying woman rather than have the child killed. Solomon then declared the woman who showed the compassion as the true mother and handed the child to her.

King Solomon demonstrates wisdom rarely seen then among leaders, as well as among today's leaders. Among Solomon's writing credits are most of the Proverbs, Songs of Solomon, and perhaps Ecclesiastes. Solomon ruled the kingdom of Israel during the era of approximately 1015 B.C. to 975 B.C. He is credited in I Kings 4:30-34 in the Bible with wisdom greater than all of the children of the east country, and all the wisdom of Egypt. He also wrote 1,005 songs (or poems).

While the book of Proverbs contrasts wisdom with eventual foolishness, Solomon spoke 3,000 proverbs, and various kings all over the earth sought out Solomon for his knowledge. It is my hope that we can take his writings and utilize them in our lives today.

How complete would your life be if I could give you the treasures of the world, and provide you with all of the "secrets" to all of the success you could ever handle in this lifetime? Would you be interested in completely understanding the mysteries of achieving the highest pinnacle in business and personal relationships? Would I have your attention if we were to sit down and discuss all of the important principles taught by a wise king, or one whose wisdom was far greater than all men, and was the most famous orator and teacher of the world in his time?

In First Kings in the Old Testament of the Bible we read about the wisdom that Solomon possessed, and how far above he was in wisdom and understanding than the average man.

The second section of the Wisdom of Solomon picks up the story of Solomon, the king who chose wisdom, and advocated that all rulers should seek wisdom from beside the throne of God in order to rule wisely and justly. Wisdom in Bible terms is defined as *God's spirit, intelligent, holy, the fashioner of all things, an emanation of God's glory, a reflection of eternal light, and an image of divine goodness.*

So what can Solomon offer us today, and is there a direct tie into living a good life and being a God-fearing person, and applying principles and the wisdom of Solomon to business operations and ethics? Yes these teachings work for day-to-day life, but what can these teachings do for us in the world of business?

It poses an interesting question and is worth the effort to study out what Solomon may provide a world of fast-paced, make as much money as possible…in any way possible, and use whatever means to keep increasing wealth and raising our status in society.

I was sitting at my home one winter morning and an idea popped into my head. The idea was to take the writings of Solomon, particularly Proverbs, and draw a correlation of how those words written over 3,000 years ago might be applicable to today in business.

Could there even be a correlation drawn to today -- with all of the chaos of daily life? We are so far more advanced as a society than the people of Solomon's time, at least in technology, medicine, and science. But are we that much more advanced in wisdom?

Take a look a few inventions, processes, and successes during the past 100 years. There are many to list, but for now it is staggering to think about the incredible advances our global society has made.

- We have computers that think faster than the human brain, however, computers have evolved much faster than the human brain. Computers have been around for only a few decades, yet rapid technological advancements have made computers faster, smaller and more powerful.

- We have upwards of 50 micro processors in an automobile, and planes that carry hundreds of people to a destination in hours, thousands of miles away, instead of days or weeks.

- We have the Internet and billions of pages of information to learn from right at our fingertips.

- We have space shuttles that take our astronauts into space and back again in a matter of days. The Space Shuttle travels at a constant speed of 17,500 per hour.

- We have ways of turning goods into profits with people in a different country, and they pay the same moment that they make a decision to purchase, with the Internet and a credit card.

- We have companies like Wal Mart that bring in $4.5 billion in one week (yes billion with a "b").

- We can hold meetings with others who might be 8,000 miles away, all in real time, and you can see them on the screen as you interact with them.

- We can cure deadly diseases and help people live normal lives that would not have been able to do so even 10 years ago.

- Credit card processing companies can process over $20 trillion (yes, trillion with a "t") in one year.

- We can see planets through a telescope – 42 light years away. To put that into perspective, one light year is equal to 5,878,625,373,183 miles (that is 5.8 trillion miles). Pretty staggering once you think about the many advances that our society has made even in the past 100 years.

So what can a king who lived 3,000 years ago teach a society that is so far advanced in its culture? What could he possibly do for us in this day and age, and could his wisdom actually assist us in our current business practices?

For starters Solomon can take us back to our humble beginnings and help us realize that although these things are wonderful inventions to make our lives better and more productive, they don't always remind us that we have a God that is providing us with so many blessings. Solomon's teachings can assist us in doing what is good, and what is right, and what can affect us for the eternities, not just in this life. *I would dare say that the Proverbs of Solomon are more applicable today that they were 3,000 years ago.*

I wrote this book with the intention that Solomon's wisdom is even more applicable in business today… but don't stop there. His wisdom continues to enlighten millions of people on all continents, and in many ways.

Solomon wrote: *To know wisdom and instruction; to perceive the words of understanding.* What is "wisdom" and why should we care to achieve it in this lifetime? Wisdom is defined as *"good sense and a wise attitude, belief, or course of action; the teachings of the ancient wise men."* To add to the "official definition", I believe wisdom is a combination of:

- maturity,

- self confidence,

- reliance upon God,

- listening to your inner feelings, and

- being mature enough to accept the feelings that you experience.

It's interesting that there is one additional word that by its very nature, will help you achieve wisdom in this life: *experience.* When we experience something, we have a baseline to form some kind of judgment about how we will act or re-act in the future. We have a reference point to look back to and remember how we reacted, or not. We will either avoid the same situation in the future, or we will embrace it and possibly even improve upon it.

We lack wisdom if we continue to make the same mistake(s) over and over. You've probably heard that one definition of insanity is to do something over and over and expect a different result. Someone with a little wisdom will stop the insanity and try something a little different, or in a different order, or add one more ingredient.

Why is Solomon perceived to be so wise? What did he do that made him the topic of discussion in First Kings where he was touted by philosophers and prophets of his day as the wisest man in the region...in all the earth? For one thing, he found out who the true mother of a child was by offering to cut the child in two pieces and give both mothers half. The "counterfeit" mother out of jealously and selfishness said that would be fine, whereas the real mother pleaded with Solomon to spare the child's life, and give it to the other woman.

It took a little wisdom to figure out who was telling the truth, and who only wanted a selfish gain for herself no matter who would be hurt in the process. Solomon called them out and made them face a difficult decision that would affect all three of them in a dramatic way.

Solomon built a vast empire. His rule and reign was so immense that it encompassed millions of acres of land; very powerful cities; trade routes that created wealth so vast that he was a billionaire by today's standards in a time when no one came close to the enormous amount of wealth that he had attained.

Solomon's empire included strategic alliances that kept his enemies at bay, and yet allowed him to freely trade with any country he wished. He controlled food sources and had enough allies in the surrounding countries, that if there were to be a famine, his people would not suffer.

This "empire" that Solomon built was the envy of all kings of the world in his day. And, this empire is the example that I wish to turn to in the study of how this king used wisdom to build his empire.

Solomon of course was human, and he had his faults and shortcomings. He was by no means a perfect little angel all of his life. No one is perfect and we all have faults. We can still learn from the imperfection of others, as well as in ourselves...I hope. But if we ever say we have learned it all, and there is nothing more to improve on, well then there is a problem, and maybe if we reach that point it's time to go on vacation. If we can't learn, and dream and hope and be curious then what is the point in going on...even living?

I am much wiser today after raising six children—all with different personalities, wants and desires. I learn each and every day that each child is different and wants to do or achieve different things in life. There are times when I wish I could just fit them into the perfect little life that my wife and I would like them to experience and achieve, but that defeats the purpose of learning and growing. We provide them with the necessities of life, a good example, and the "track to run on". Some choose to run in the fast lane, while others may hold back and wish to see how the rest of us roll out life.

Let's get back to **the wisdom that we need today**. Achieving business wisdom is also knowing that you have a short term tactical plan with immediate, measurable results that will roll up to a long term strategy.

The long term strategy must fit with the short term plan. The tactics plug into a cohesive, tight action plan that make up the successful overall plan. It's like a mathematics equation…8 X 3 = 24; and 3 X 8 = 24; and 24 ÷ 8 = 3. They fit together so that the answer is the same no matter how you change it up. *Tactics and strategies* need to work in the same fashion.

To know instruction then is to listen to experts in their field and mold their tutoring in to your set of circumstances and solutions. We are constantly learning (at least I'm assuming you are still interested in the concept of learning) and applying the valuable tidbits of information into our own set of circumstances.

I am still learning from my children and many situations in business each day. I learn things from my wife each day that makes me a better person. I learn from business colleagues and situations in business that all serve to provide volumes of information and processes to follow. I learn from catching up on the news that people will do just about anything to move ahead as they exercise selfish dominion.

We each have the opportunity to bless the lives of others and ask for divine intervention to help us along the way. You and I can make a profound difference in the lives of others and reach out and lift them up in ways we have probably not even thought of. It all begins with a belief that we as human beings have something good to offer, and that there are people in need at our work, in our church, in our neighborhood, in our country, and

> ### Key Point
>
> You and I can make a profound difference in the lives of others and reach out and lift them up in ways we have probably not even thought of.

yes, in the world.

We have a lot to cover in this book and we should get started on this brief journey of learning more about wisdom. So sit back and enjoy a correlation of the teachings and writings of Solomon, and how his wisdom is still alive and helping out millions of people throughout the world.

CHAPTER TWO

Wisdom and Instruction of Proverbs

*Good actions give strength to ourselves and
inspire good actions in others.*

- Plato

Keys to Proverbs

Proverbs is one of the few Biblical books that clearly spells out its purpose: *To provide wisdom and instruction.* The words **wisdom** and **instruction** in Proverbs 1:2 complement each other because **wisdom** (hokhmah) means "skill" and **instruction** (musar) means "discipline." No skill is perfected without discipline, and when a person has skill he has freedom to create something marvelous. Proverbs deals with the most fundamental skill of all: practical righteousness before God in every area of life.

In its original version, Proverbs was written and compiled by Solomon between his reign in about 1015 B.C. to 975 B.C. Then the verses contained in chapters 25-29 were added to the book in 720 B.C.

The great underlying theme of the book of Proverbs is that *true wisdom is centered in respect and reverence for God.* And, although

> **Profound Quote**
>
> *"When I was a boy of fourteen, my father was so ignorant I could hardly stand to have the old man around. But when I got to be twenty-one, I was astonished at how much the old man had learned in seven years."*
>
> **-- Mark Twain**

the book gives us remarkable passages on wisdom, it must be noted that these are not absolute guarantees. We should not be tempted to take these wise sayings and turn them into literal promises. For example, it is generally true that those who keep God's commandments will enjoy length of days and long life (Proverbs 3:2). But this should not be interpreted as an ironclad guarantee of living a long life.

The simple fact that we can make wise decisions not to drink and drive; not to smoke; not to be involved in criminal activity; all make us the wiser person and can prolong our days. The important thing to remember is that it is important to keep God's commandments no matter how long we have here on the earth.

Let's take a brief journey down the path of Personal Development and spend some time on a few areas of interest that we should give some attention to. The topics that I refer to will help each of us in laying a foundation of considerable strength as we roll out the best possible strategy for developing true wisdom and building a successful empire.

Solomon was blessed with *wisdom and knowledge exceeding much,* and over the span of four decades he built a massive empire as the King of Israel. He took steps to ensure that his empire was built in an orderly, yet rapid pace, all the while keeping his focus on a couple of key objectives: 1). building a temple for God; 2). building his own empire; 3) forming allies that would strengthen his empire in case of conflict or economic downturn.

I would like to open your mind to 12 Key Principles that Solomon concentrated heavily on as he built his empire. Although these 12 Key Principles are not entirely inclusive of the lessons taught throughout the book of Proverbs, they are a representation of the important areas of critical focus that we need to adhere to as we build our own empires. They are the principles that I have learned as I have studied Solomon. Here are the categories:

12 Keys to Building a Successful Empire

    I.   **Seek Wisdom**

    II.   **Provide Clarity**

    III.   **Develop Strategic Alliances**

    IV.   **Look for Opportunities**

    V.   **Stay Focused**

    VI.   **Purge Conflicts and Train Your Leaders**

    VII. **Hold Others Accountable**

    VIII. **Seek Prosperity and Expect to Win**

    IX.   **Avoid Over Spending and Control Costs**

    X.   **Exercise Integrity**

    XI.   **Communicate**

    XII. **Exercise Common Sense**

Let's examine the wisdom in Solomon's approach to building an empire. There are many elements to building a successful empire, but for now we will just focus on 12 of them. Through his actions Solomon defined how to build a successful empire. These steps can be broken out into elements that proved successful for Solomon, and in this discussion, the 12 Keys to Building a Successful Empire are as follows:

I. Seek Wisdom

Solomon requested to have greater wisdom bestowed upon him to make good decisions, and help lead God's people. His request was granted because his speech pleased the Lord. You and I, and any leader for that matter can have the same permission granted. Why not...? All men are created equal, so why can't we all be given wisdom to lead? I believe we all can receive this approval if we ask with a humble intention as Solomon did.

The first key to building anything worthwhile is to connect with someone who can open doors for you. Typically we look to someone that we know of to help open doors and there is nothing wrong with this. I believe that people are placed in our path to help us out in times of our lives. These people may not even know that they quite possibly could have been sent by God to help us out.

When engaged in the process of connecting with others, we are also connecting to a higher source, and that higher source for me is God. This connection is the first step to take in building an empire. Whether we need someone to help us with connections to launch our business; a connection to funding; or a connection to a key supplier; or even a connection to a key partner to help launch a new venture, or product, *the key is connecting.*

I would like you to consider that there are higher powers at work that can be a strong force for each of us. There is a higher power in whom you can rely on to ask for wisdom as you lead. It all begins there. Since this takes action on our part, we start the process by *doing.* We don't necessarily need to know **what** we seek; instead we must know **how to connect** with a source that can affect our learning and become a rainmaker to open the way.

I realize I'm going out on a controversial limb here, but it needs to be said: Leaders of organizations must take a deeper look into their treasure trove of wisdom, and ask for better intuition and instinct to make sound decisions. Make that connection with God.

The United States of America was founded on the principle that a belief in a Supreme Being and acting upon that belief, was paramount in building a newly formed country and government. The Founding

Fathers of the U.S. were by no means perfect, but they were God-fearing leaders who sought His wisdom on a consistent basis.

Some people in influential positions seem to reject the notion of endorsing religion in government and business institutions. Why…? When we make decisions we usually do so based on our instinct, or gut feeling. It's important to recognize that without our instinct or intuition, few noteworthy ideas would rise from our leaders, or from us. *Instinct* or *intuition* is a divine process as much as it is intellectual, and these are primary sources for seeking wisdom.

I will talk more of the type of resources needed to build an empire later. For now let it suffice that we can narrow the resources down to these two categories:

1. Asking for Wisdom, and
2. Taking Action.

For some people however, once they connect with God, after time they no longer feel compelled to seek His counsel. I have fallen into this trap as well, and have lived to regret it. I'm not quite sure why we stop seeking wisdom from a higher source, or from others, but once that connection is made, over time our finite minds seem to somehow feel the mystery is over. How sad to think that there is nothing more. But there is. There is much more to consider, and much more counsel to follow.

Thank goodness we can find the answers to previously unanswered questions and we know the right action to take in given circumstances. In this knowledge, we gain ultimate fulfillment, and if we aspire to be great leaders, we must first be emotionally and spiritually fulfilled. We then will be in a position to lead and be a true mentor to those that will follow.

What is truly exciting is that God offers this question to each of us when we learn to seek His counsel – instead of satisfying our own egos. When we connect with God and trade our ego-based selfishness for a position of submission and doing right in God's eyes, we then enjoy the opportunity to ask for the means to further our aspirations the most. If we are to build a "kingdom", or "realm", or "empire" we must do this.

Solomon asked for wisdom and knowledge. He requested of God, in prayer, *"Give me now wisdom and knowledge, that I may go out and come in before this people; for who can rule this great people of Thine?"* What did Solomon ask for? Glory… Riches…Conquests…a Harem of women…Longevity…Fame? No. He asked, humbly, for wisdom and knowledge. Solomon showed **Humility** and **Wisdom in his request. These are two very important ingredients for leaders to possess in order to build a sustainable empire.**

Remember that building an empire requires that you have followers…and that people follow leaders in whom they believe and actually like. When our own ego gets in the way, humility and reliance on seeking God's wisdom is often times tossed out of the window. People don't like to follow someone who is arrogant, and who only thinks of their own benefit, rather than the good of the team. Don't fall into this trap.

What do most people ask for? Riches; Fame; Glory; Trouble-Free Life; Youth; Better Health; Bigger House; More Toys; etc. Would our lives be any different if we humbled ourselves and asked for *wisdom* and *knowledge*? Would our lives feel less encumbered if we actually took the time to seek wisdom from God and ask Him what he wants us to do?

Being humble does not mean that you are weak. In fact a humble person is compared to an exalted person; one who respects others. Some of the most humble people I have learned from are actually very powerful and persuasive leaders. Many people follow these humble leaders because of their concern and understanding for their constituents. It is more of a higher connection, and leaders who possess the quality of humility, can command thousands, even millions to follow them simply through their example.

I am absolutely convinced that if we do this, doors will be opened unto to us and we will see with more clarity what is actually best for us, and those that we lead. Yet, this is one of the more difficult things to do in this life, because we feel like we can do it on our own, and we enjoy our independence.

God recognized Solomon's humility and concern for others, and blessed him with additional knowledge and riches. Our own leaders today could learn a thing or two from Solomon's request. Solomon did not approach God from a position of personal gain; he approached God from a position of humility, honor, and service. His position was to look at how he might serve in the best manner possible.

In return for Solomon's eager desire to please God and seek his wisdom first, with a simple request to gain wisdom and knowledge and lead God's people, Solomon received wisdom and knowledge— as well as riches, wealth, honor, and victory over his enemies. *The lesson in this is that God sometimes delivers more than we ask for when our approach is from a position of humility, awe, respect, and service.*

II. Provide Clarity

A detailed story of how Solomon ruled on a dispute between two women who claimed the same son is the beginning of proof of Solomon's wisdom. After hearing both sides of the story, Solomon took decisive action and provided a clear picture to both women of what he was prepared to do. Dividing the baby in two halves was a grisly solution, but he was very clear of what was about to happen since there were two opposing narratives of whose son it was. *It is important to build an empire through*

> **Key Point**
>
> It is important to build an empire through integrity, ruling in fairness, honesty, being true to our commitments, and providing clarity.

integrity, ruling in fairness, honesty, being true to our commitments, and providing clarity. Solomon's reputation preceded him as wise and fair with his constituency.

Many leaders today want to ensure that their decisions are correct before they act. This is virtually impossible to achieve in a world full of imperfect information and loads of uncertainty. Sometimes critical decisions are postponed and clear objectives become unrealized, instead of setting a clear course to follow. When this happens leaders provide vague and hesitant direction to their teams and simply hope their subordinates figure out the answers along the way. The problem with this is that the leader and the subordinate hardly ever line up their expectations with the end result. One has a certain set of strategies to follow, while the other has set their own course in their mind, and the two sets of ideals rarely meet.

Leaders today want to be accurate in their assessments of critical situations, and then again accurate in the delivery of their answers. However, as leaders we must clarify our position and make it clear what we expect the outcome to be. If we don't know the outcome, then tell your people with proper planning comes targeted execution. Efficiencies are adhered to and effective communication takes place to achieve the anticipated outcome. As leaders we must make *clarity* more important than being accurate.

Subordinates will learn more from leaders when they make decisions and take decisive action, instead of waiting for the stars to align. Too many managers today will analyze a situation to death, and experience *decision constipation.* They are so consumed with the thought of possibly failing that they fail to make a decision, because if they make a decision it could be the wrong one, and if it's the wrong one they might get fired—oh no! Take a deep breath and use common sense (more on this in a minute).

Lee Iacocca, former CEO and Chairman of Chrysler Corporation was a master of making decisions and standing by his beliefs and values. I don't always agree with him on politics, but you have to love his management style and how he does what he says he will do. He doesn't mince words, and he gets the job done.

Mr. Iacocca lived through the depression, which hit his family hard. The stories go that he gets upset about waste, whether it's throwing away food, having to get rid of clothing just because it's gone out of style, or waste in business is a direct result of the depression. In the back of his mind he knows disaster could strike without warning.

In 1978 Mr. Iacocca joined Chrysler after a successful career with Ford. It didn't take long for him to figure out that Chrysler was in a state of emergency. There was a serious lack of communication, and there was no teamwork. Each department seemed to be working in a vacuum. He had to make some drastic decisions. He was forced to fire many of the executives. He tried to set up a partnership between Chrysler and Volkswagen, but Volkswagen realized how deep in debt Chrysler was and the deal fell through. Mr. Iacocca was not able to pull everything together and make it work, and he had to go to the government to get government-backed loans. He also bargained with the union for cuts in salary and benefits. He reduced his salary to $1.00 per year to show that everyone at the company must be willing to sacrifice if their company was to survive. He was able to understand the worker as well as the executives, and somehow pull them together. By 1983 Mr. Iacocca had Chrysler back on their feet, and on July 13, 1983 Chrysler paid back all their government loans that totaled over $800 million. He made a public statement, "We at Chrysler borrow money the old fashioned way. We pay it back."

If the decision we make in the spirit of pronouncing clarity turns out to be incorrect after additional information becomes available, change plans and explain why. It is our job as leaders to make decisions, and sometimes take risks—that is what we are paid to do. If we need to adjust our course then do it quickly. The cost to us is a ding on our pride. The cost to the company of not taking action is paralysis.

In Solomon's day, people came to him with their concerns and he had a good reputation for judging fairly with them to administer justice. The people saw that the wisdom of God was in Solomon, and they feared him, but they also respected him as a leader who could take decisive action. He not only showed compassion for the true mother of the living child, and he also repeated their account back to them to make sure he fully understood what was going on. Through clarity he then told them the solution – as he saw it, to the problem. The moment that his clear thoughts were expressed to the two women, the true mother was revealed. Would he have actually cut the baby in two pieces? Possibly. The answer to that question is not important. What is important is that we know by providing clarity to the situation, the truth was revealed.

How often do we as leaders repeat the problem back to our employees, or children, or colleagues? How often do we provide clarity to the situation and seek feedback? How often do we worry more about being accurate over providing clarity? Too many leaders today suppose that they have it all figured out, and that others in the organization should just trust that they know what they are doing—since they are in a position of authority. As leaders, we must exercise more clarity in our communication, and worry less about always being accurate.

Here are five simple steps to remember as you work with others to provide clarity of the situation:

1. Clarify your position.

2. Seek Feedback.

3. Assess your options.

4. Make a decision.

5. Make adjustments when and if necessary.

III. Develop Strategic Alliances

You have heard me say this before if you have read any of my other books, or have attended one of my seminars. In order for you to succeed in business, *you will need to form strategic alliances with other people, and other companies.* Solomon made strategic alliances with friendly kings and queens to increase resources and insure clear trade routes, and establish power. Strategic alliances can also increase cooperation and eliminate competition.

The first significant alliance Solomon built was with Pharaoh of Egypt, when he took Pharaoh's daughter and brought her to the city of David. This act not only gained an alliance to the south, but also made available precious resources from Egypt. This marriage alliance opened a trade route through Africa, and kept war with Egypt away from Solomon's kingdom. It was a brilliant move and allowed the Kingdom of Israel to grow stronger during a time of peace rather than during a time of war.

Solomon also needed the Cedars of Lebanon to build his temple and his palace. These Cedars were highly sought after resources in his day, and Solomon created a way to obtain them. By going it alone he would have limited labor and other resources to succeed in his mission of building a magnificent temple. Once he partnered with others who had available laborers, resources, and teamwork, Solomon realized he could achieve far more of his goals in much less time.

He made a pact with the Lebanese King Hiram of Tyre, trading oil, wine, barley, and wheat for woodsmen, metal workers, and various craftsmen, along with Lebanese timber.

Solomon then continued to build and strengthen his kingdom over the next two decades. One of his more notable alliances was with Makeda, Queen of Sheba (who ruled over Ethiopia during a time where Ethiopian power controlled Africa during the era of 970 BC).

In Solomon's day, Makeda's importance was trading through the route known as the "Horn" of Africa. Egyptian hieroglyphic records indicate that the Pharaohs obtained frankincense and myrrh from Ethiopia, and from the Somali coast, as far back as 2700 BC. Ethiopia was a much larger kingdom in the days of Sheba, spanning from the Red Sea to the modern day Zimbabwe.

Solomon studied history and learned this from the alliance several hundred years earlier between King Rameses II of Egypt and Queen Nefertari of Africa, which at that time had ended a 100-year war between Egypt and Nubia.

Solomon also formed alliances with the Arabian Kings, and many other neighboring countries, which virtually guaranteed him peace and prosperity during his rule. *The strategy of cooperation vs. competition proved to be highly successful in an area of the world where no one has trusted any other empire in the region for thousands of years.*

It is essential to have strong, open, powerful flow of trade in any empire, and Solomon was well aware of the resources surrounding his kingdom. So we have to acknowledge that opening a flow of trade to obtain resources, skills, and information from other empires is critical to leading a successful empire.

The same applies in business today. If an enterprise cannot trade products and services, they fail. This is also true with countries, as demonstrated by the fall of the economy in Argentina in 2006. As of this writing, Cuba also remains in a state of early 1960's economic stagnation as a result of the American embargo against Fidel Castro. A quick study of the economy and the 30-40 year old cars Cuban citizens drive, illustrates how inadequate the country truly is without strategic trade partners. Although as you study the stagnation of the economy, it is clear how Cuban production seems to have stopped in the 1950's as a result of the trade barriers imposed against Cuba.

As of this writing, Hugo Chavez, president of Venezuela is presently on the same path of dictatorship, and is leading his country into shambles just as all other dictators throughout the world before him have done. What he has failed to realize is when people can't even get the basic staples of life like bread, eggs, milk and other food supplies, they rebel and actually step up and do something about it. "Less than 40 percent of consumer demand is being met for at least 10 basic food items as Venezuelans struggle with shortages that have been partly blamed on price controls," explained Finance Minister Rodrigo Cabezas as he related the story to the Associated Press in December 2007.

"The government lifted price controls on some types of milk. Finding milk has become especially difficult for Venezuelans, and the government estimates the meager supply of milk is meeting only 10 percent of consumer demand."

Chavez imposed price controls in 2003 to keep a cap on inflation, but prices continued to rise amid a briskly growing economy and heavy government spending bankrolled by soaring oil profits. Inflation surged to 4.4 percent in one month alone, sending annual inflation in 2007 to 18.6%.

Many foods covered by the price controls -- sugar, cooking oil, milk, black beans, eggs and fresh chicken -- were hard to find in supermarkets, and Chavez's critics warned that shortages were likely to persist as long as the controls were maintained. Economists say milk is also especially scarce because of a lack of production in Venezuela. (*Source: Fabiola Sanchez, Associated Press Writer, December 2007.*)

With little to no significant trading partners the country cannot supply proper goods and services to it citizens. Somehow Mr. Chavez assumes he does not need key trade partners for food, clothing, water, power…you know the basic elements of sustaining life.

Call me crazy, but aligning your self with weapons trading partners, and nuclear arms dealers probably should be moved down the list a notch or two. Unless you're planning on doing what all good dictators do today: hate America…have an overwhelming desire to take over the world…keep your people in utterly depressed conditions so that they have no choice but to go with your regime…and eventually throw your country into economic ruin.

However, on the other hand…forming strategic alliances to move the cause of "good" forward is a lot more productive, and requires much less energy.

I really have never understood the selfish pride of dictators, and how they can personally live in the lap of serious luxury – while their own people suffer as trade with other nations is cut off. Just keep this in mind as we learn the basic rules and guidelines about trade: *Trade among other empires is vital to any empire's success.*

IV. Look for Opportunities

Solomon wanted to build the most magnificent structure of his time for his God. He looked for an opportunity to please God by constructing a temple where the holy priests could worship and make sacrifices. Solomon's mission of building a temple was a massive undertaking, and an opportunity for him to please God. Israel did not have enough stone, gold, wood, or workers to begin work. Solomon gathered resources, formed trade with other empires, and bartered possessions he could spare for the resources he needed to complete the mission.

Solomon gathered his resources, gathered together an army of chariots and horsemen and stationed them in strategic cities. He brought his horses and chariots from other countries, such as Egypt and Kue, then sold many to other countries and built his own fleet of chariots by profiting from the trade.

Many manufacturing and distribution empires of today build masses of resources, and then consolidate them into hubs and thus further their influence throughout their empire. Delta Airlines follows this system of "hubs" that cut down on costs and make travel more efficient for their bottom line. It is not as efficient for the traveler to get from Seattle, WA to Charlotte, North Carolina. However, with a hubs in Salt Lake City and Atlanta, the airline is able to carry 300 plus people on one giant 767 from Salt Lake City to Atlanta, and then have the traveler take a commuter flight from Atlanta to Charlotte, with 20-30 people.

Delta has created this hub system in three major cities: Salt Lake City, Atlanta and Cincinnati to keep costs low and efficiency high. They also have partnered with regional airlines to provide the services at the gate and on board the plane – while Delta provides the equipment.

Also, as an update, the recent merger of Delta Airlines and Northwest Airlines creates another hub in Minneapolis that will reduce flights through Cincinnati. I'm not going to try to keep up with the latest mergers and acquisitions, I just want to illustrate how this hub system works in modern times as well as in Solomon's day. Delta is one example of a corporation that is constantly looking for opportunities to become more efficient and effective in their business structure.

On another front, in order to build the temple and make it structurally sound, Solomon needed wood and stone. He approached Hiram, King of Tyre, to barter wood and skilled workers in exchange for barley, wheat, wine, and oil. Solomon learned that he had 150,000+ laborers at his disposal within his own center of influence. This would be equivalent to employing all of the employees at Microsoft, and the number one business in the world Exxon Mobile, combined for a period of twenty years.

Another example of looking for opportunities is found with Children's Miracle Network (CMN). CMN is one of the finest charitable causes in the world focused on fund raising for children's hospitals. The organization is made up of a cohesive team of 135 people at the national office; 176 children's hospitals; 120 corporate partners; and over 350 media partners – all with one goal in mind: raise as much as possible to help improve the lives of sick and injured children.

I bring up this example as I have seen first hand how each different constituent is constantly looking for opportunities to partner with other entities to achieve the goal: *raise more funds for sick and injured kids*. As I have worked with this great charity over the past five years, seeking out additional opportunities is a constant focus.

Keeping our eye on the primary focus of raising funds for children also requires ingenuity and innovation, which in turn requires a conscience effort of looking for other opportunities.

> **Key Point**
>
> Keeping our eye on the primary focus requires ingenuity and innovation, which in turn requires a conscience effort of looking for other opportunities.

When forced to look at other innovative options due to a difficult economy, I asked the Development team at CMN to look at what they do best, (connect corporate sponsors with their employees and customers to raise funds for children's hospitals) and then to come up with some strategic, innovative ideas to look for new programs. Once armed with this idea, the sky has been the limit in coming up with creative, effective and efficient ways of raising funds with a variety of programs. In one year the total amount raised jumped by $10 million dollars by strategizing and executing on a three new programs.

That was not the end by any means: new partnerships were formed and current partnerships were strengthened. And, since this process works with for-profits and non-profits alike, we should ask ourselves:

- How is your organization doing in seeking out opportunities?

- What new innovations await your participation?

- What new programs, products or services are waiting to be born within your own organization?

They are out there, and an afternoon spent brainstorming with your team, your Board, your advisors and your suppliers can help you figure out what the next innovative product, service or program should be.

Solomon expanded his empire to be the most powerful trading and military force in the world. He was constantly seeking out opportunities to align his country with other countries to benefit the trading prowess of his nation. *Make certain that you train your executives, managers and employees to seek out new opportunities. Provide incentives to those who come up with new, innovative, efficient ways to make your organization better.*

V. Stay Focused

Solomon decided to build a temple for the Lord, and a royal palace for himself. The construction of a temple with all of its extravagance was indeed a major undertaking. Again, Solomon kept his focus on how he might please God with his actions. The Children of Israel had been worshipping God in a portable temple as they moved through the wilderness. Solomon believed that God deserved to be worshipped in a solid, ornate, and holy structure.

Solomon's vision was extravagant and would require elements from other parts of the world to be brought in. Although he did not have these elements close by, *his focus was not deterred by these obstacles.* Solomon realized that he needed to rely on others to help him accomplish this lofty goal of constructing an edifice worthy of an offering—even a place worthy of accepting a visit from God.

> **Definition**
>
> **Focus**: a center of activity, attraction, or attention; a point of concentration.

Have you ever seen the poster that shows a setting sun on the horizon, and placed in front of the setting sun are four large boulders in the ocean. The caption of the poster is "When you take your eyes off the goal, all you see are the obstacles." The primary point is that the obstacles of deep, cold waters; and large objects standing in the way, are usually what we humans focus on first, rather than seeing past those obstacles and focusing on the beauty of the setting sun.

The primary mission of empires today is to generate as much revenue as possible while controlling costs, which leads to more equity or profit. There are a myriad of obstacles introduced on a daily basis that threaten the primary vision of any institution, large or small. The distractions can and do become overwhelming and drain the energy, sometimes the life out of the organization and its members.

Too many distractions creep in the *empires* of today, and rob them of achieving their potential. The poor economy…slow or no sales…competition launching a new product…employee relations and human resource challenges…internal strife with managers…and a thousand other things. The key is to remain focused on who you are and what you do.

A great example of staying focused is the founding of the United States of America. The U.S. has been blessed with many individuals who stayed focused to accomplish the mission they set out achieve. This country was founded on the principles that Almighty God is the Supreme Being that may be worshipped whenever, and however one chooses.

Solomon, and the Founding Fathers of the United States of America, in their wisdom, kept their focus, and chose to honor God. They focused on a primary mission that could not escape their ever – waking thoughts and actions. Nothing stood in the way of their mission and they vigorously planned and implemented strategies to accomplish their goals. They sacrificed their fortunes, their fame, their property, and even their lives to stay focused on their primary mission: to create a sovereign nation free from the oppressions of a tyrannical leader.

Likewise, Solomon recognized *"who is able to build a house for*

Him (God), for the heavens and the highest heavens cannot contain him. Solomon's temple, his primary focus and mission, made other buildings look rather gaunt and dull in comparison…good grief, the walls were even lined with gold! This undertaking was considered very industrious and Solomon had to build a work force large enough to match the ambitious goal of building a temple that would rival any structure on earth in beauty and magnitude. Solomon's task force required twenty years to complete the mission, and staying focused on accomplishing this mission was the highest priority for him and his staff.

I will be the first to admit that that sometimes it can be difficult to stay focused on what matters most. However when you are truly committed to something, distractions can be managed and even ignored to bring about the completion of your task. Think of the following 7 principles in staying focused. They may not all work for you, but I have found that when you follow these principles, you stay focused, and you are able to direct your positive energies to the task at hand.

1. **Establish well-defined goals** – your goals are the foundation of your plan and your plan is the roadmap to lead you to your destiny. Setting goals in not a new concept, but it is a wise principle to use and a habit that you should establish. Remember a goal not written is only a wish.

2. **Create and stick to a priority list** – sometimes a simple list of priorities can keep you focused on what needs to be accomplished – and when. I like to have a priority list to refer to when distractions enter the picture…it keeps me…*focused.*

3. **Track and Report your progress** – Remember this: *what gets reported gets done.* Whether you are reporting to your self or to the board, when you are able to track your progress and show how you reach certain milestones, you can keep on the straight path without deviations.

4. **Break tasks into smaller pieces** – a big project can look so overwhelming at times. I have found that when you take the big picture and break it down to smaller elements, individual pieces don't seem as daunting, and each time you complete one of the smaller tasks it is invigorating and empowering.

5. **Reward yourself** – you need to give yourself a pat on the back once in a while and reward yourself for your discipline. That can be as simple as blocking out time for you to read a book; see a movie; go out to dinner; go on a vacation; or watch your favorite sitcom.

6. **Visualize the end result** – Constantly seeing the end result in your mind is a great motivator. Visualize what you want to accomplish. If the end result is truly important to you, it can serve as a powerful reminder that your sacrifices along the way will be worth it.

7. **Ask for help** – Unless you have a big red and yellow "S" stamped on the chest of your blue spandex uniform, I would suggest that you reach out to others once in a while and ask for help. The cool thing about asking for help is that it shows a little humanness, and people really do like to help others. They don't mind helping you because they can share a little expertise and provide a little compassion to others...we humans, for the most part, are just wired that way.

VI. Purge Conflicts and Train Your Leaders

Solomon lived during a period of extreme conflict, distrust, warfare, and backstabbing. Hmmmm, doesn't sound too far off from the world we live in today! Solomon quickly learned that he needed to be the primary leader in the eyes of the people to provide vision and direction. He needed to do away with two of his sources of strife, who had laid false claim to the throne prior to his father David's passing.

By eliminating sources of strife, Solomon was able to focus on his mission and accomplish what he originally set out to do. Shimei was an enemy of his father David, and Solomon made a move against Shimei to force him into making a treaty. If Shimei broke that pact, he would be eliminated from the kingdom and face execution.

Even though Shimei was an enemy of King David and a threat to the throne, Solomon allowed him to build a house in the region. He was commanded not to depart from a general territory near Jerusalem for any reason, or he would face certain death. Shimei agreed to this arrangement. Three years later, however, Shimei's servants left the area and Shimei followed them to Gath, thus violating his agreement with Solomon. Solomon's rule dictated prompt execution for Shimei. This act strengthened Solomon's leadership and gave him absolute authority over his people.

I certainly don't recommend executing insubordinate employees, but I do recommend good old-fashioned communication, and a chance to discuss the problem with them. If things don't improve you can help them move on to the next level of their career, outside of your empire.

I am also not advocating that you *eliminate* your biggest opponents, but that you take a careful watch to eliminate strife in your empire, and to take control of it early on.

If there are people in your "empire" grasping for your power, you have two choices:

1. Make them allies or
2. Send them away if you are to have absolute authority.

Good leaders create an aura of confidence that they will lead the people to victory. It is when the people feel confident of their leader's ability to remove obstacles and develop an atmosphere of teamwork, that they make special things happen. If the team does not buy into the leader's ability to lead them, morale suffers and victory it is only a distant whisper.

Developing leaders in your organization is a crucial step to becoming a truly great enterprise. The challenge is to choose leaders that check their ego's at the door, and put the organization, or empire, at the forefront of their work. Leaders are those rare individuals that can clearly articulate the vision and direction of the organization, and have their constituents buy into that vision.

Training your leaders to respect your authority can be as simple as explaining the rules, holding them accountable, and exercising humility in your approach. ***In many cases that also means that after you do all of these steps, then simply get out of their way and let them perform.***

The next step—holding others accountable—might resolve some of the challenges of strife and lack of ancillary leadership in your empire.

VII. Hold Others Accountable

King Solomon was able to clearly articulate his vision to his subordinates through his leaders that he had chosen. Obviously, Shimei paid the ultimate price for his insubordination, but Solomon had no other choice than to hold him accountable for his actions.

It is always a good practice for leaders to care about the well being and improvement of those that they lead. It's o.k. for leaders to have a compassionate side to them and show their followers that they do care about their welfare. ***The key though, is to be able to separate wanting to be popular with direct reports vs. holding them accountable.***

Most of us try to avoid major disagreements with close friends and associates that we have worked with for a long time. When we have close friends and family members in the organization that report to us, it is sometimes difficult to strike the right balance of accountability. Even the slightest hesitation in holding others accountable can be a potential disaster waiting to happen. For one, if others feel like someone is getting special preferential treatment; the avalanche of negativity can be disastrous and extremely time consuming.

The other area gets us back to letting things slide for a while and maybe they will work themselves out if we don't take any action. This is not only dangerous thinking, it shows no leadership.

Good leaders provide the vision and direction of where the organization is headed, and then they must hold direct reports accountable to achieve the results that were agreed to.

On a football team, there are three primary aspects of achieving victory: 1) Offensive scoring; 2) Defensive prowess and holding your opponents from scoring; and 3) Special teams that do their jobs. Each player on the field relies on the other players and coaches to do their jobs. They hold each other accountable by stating the obvious: *"We are doing our job to stop the other team's offense, so defense make sure you stop them from scoring...and special teams, don't have a let down and make mistakes."*

When a coach or player holds others accountable for their actions, execution is better; members of the team are safer and less prone to injury; and ultimately victory is achieved – in most cases.

The same holds true for the other players as they pick up their side of the equation, and make things come together for a victory. In short, they expect everyone else to perform their role and they hold each other accountable to do their job.

Ask yourself the following questions and take some time to ponder how you are doing in your organization:

- Are you reluctant to give negative feedback to your direct reports?

- Do you water down negative feedback to make it more palatable?

- Does it bother you to the point of being handicapped or distracted if you feel like others are unhappy with you?

- Do you just allow problems to work themselves out, hoping you will not have to confront someone about it?

If you answered yes to any of these questions, then you need to re-evaluate how you are leading your team, and change your thinking.

As a leader you will be held accountable by the actions of your direct reports. The Board will ultimately hold you accountable as well. Make certain you drive this point home in building your empire and hold others accountable to the standards that you have established. And, remember,

The Capstone to a great plan is Accountability.

VIII. Seek Prosperity, and Expect to Win

Everything we could possibly wish for has been placed within our reach. I believe that it was intended by our Creator, that everyone who wants to live an abundant life can do so if he or she chooses. Solomon was not bashful about seeking for prosperity and using his influence to create jobs and ornate structures. In the process he also acquired key strategic alliances who assisted him in his quest to become a great leader.

I do not believe for a minute that our Creator expects us to be scrawny, uneducated, undernourished, deprived and unhappy creatures, or that He intends for us to live in want, sickness, fear, ignorance and insecurity. I do believe that God expects us to use our talents, and stay busy working for a cause and exercise our minds and bodies to the fulfillment of our dreams. He knows that times will be difficult, but I believe He expects us to keep pushing and continue working to create something of value. After all did God not bless Solomon with great prosperity?

There is enough for all to share and take a part in. Think of all of the resources that we have at our disposal: the Internet, telephones, electricity, heat, sunlight, land, air, minerals, coal, forests, oil, water and soil.

Also think of the resources in our own personalities that lie buried and mostly unused. It is stated by highly talented and mostly accurate scientists that most people only use 10% of their brains. What if we were to tap into even that next level of 10% and utilize even 2% more of our brain capacity? What amazing things would we dream up?!

Why should we expect to be rewarded less in other areas of life? An investment in our own character and education will pay us back a hundred, maybe even a thousand times over. Every pound of energy that we put into building our character and our educational foundation will pay us back immensely.

The essence of seeking prosperity lies in the notion that ***we must believe in having prosperity***. We must think of prosperity and raise our sights for greater accomplishments and not allow ourselves to think of failing. We must think success, and live success, and work for success. There is no such thing as a lack of opportunity. It was never intended that some become beggars, or stand in the unemployment line, or go bankrupt. These things usually come about because of personal decisions that we make. If we work towards our goals with all our hearts, failure should never even be an afterthought. It was never intended that we should be poor, or afraid, or worried, or unable to pay our bills when we are surrounded by prosperity merely for the taking.

It's when we think of fear and failure, well then, that is what we will get. We need to keep our thoughts on strength, good health, and riches. If our thoughts of yesterday will become the achievements of today and tomorrow, doesn't it behoove us to think only the best thoughts of success?

What price do you want to place on yourself…a hundred; a thousand; a million; ten million, a billion? Whatever price you want to set upon yourself, life will give back to you.

We can turn our thoughts into reality based on what we consume our minds with. If we think of fear and failure and worries and negative attitudes, what do you think we will receive? Yet if we consume our thoughts with positive attitudes and winning, and success, and prosperity, that is what we will get back. We must get to the point that we believe that if we control our thoughts, we will control our circumstances.

Since we are surrounded with prosperity we must learn to reach for it. Thoughts are energy, which produces more energy that produces results and achievement. When we allow ourselves to think negatively about just maintaining keeping our heads above water, or we think about competition and hard times, we allow our fears to take over and crush our confidence. Even when we don't receive the recognition that we feel we deserve from our peers, and focus more on the worry that they must think I am not doing my best, it zaps our energy.

Most of us at some point get caught up in this attitude once in a while as well, and it is wasted energy. *The key is to quickly turn negative thoughts to the off position, and focus on achievement and success.*

Before we can receive prosperity we must fix in our mind on what we want, and then concentrate all of our attention on that one thing and go out and achieve it.

One thing that we have is a memory bank full of successes that we should constantly call on and bring to the forefront of our mind. Take for example the time I read a newspaper article that stated that I would not figure in the top sprinters in the state of Utah since I was more interested in baseball and football. For the next four weeks my only thoughts were proving the reporter and all those that had read the article wrong. I would not only prove them wrong I would break

> ### Key Point
>
> Before we can receive prosperity we must fix in our mind on what we want, and then concentrate all of our attention on that one thing and go out and achieve it.

the 100 meter and 200 meter records for the entire state. My thoughts were my actions: I won both races by commanding leads, and 29 years later one of those records has never been broken. The other record stood for 24 years.

When you are *"In the Zone"*, it is referred to as a metaphor used in sports reserved for anyone that hungers and thirsts for success. Anyone can reach the zone and when they do things just fall into place – it's like being on autopilot. Being in the Zone is "the mental state of operation in which the person is fully immersed in what he or she is doing by a feeling of energized focus, full involvement, and success in the process of the activity. Colloquial terms for this or similar mental states include: to be on the ball, in the zone, or in the groove." (Source: Wikipedia, 2009)

One example of this concept is found from the story of the Formula One driver Ayrton Senna, who during qualifying for the 1988 Monaco Grand Prix explained what it was like being in the zone: *"I was already on pole, and I just kept going. Suddenly I was nearly two seconds faster than anybody else, including my teammate with the same car. And suddenly I realized that I was no longer driving the car consciously. I was driving it by a kind of instinct, only I was in a different dimension. It was like I was in a tunnel."*

When skills to compete against challenges are at the same time above average, a largely positive experience emerges. Also vital to being in the zone is a sense of control, or a state of which seems effortless and masterful. Control and concentration are at their highest levels and go beyond the point of normal awareness.

So how do you achieve this transcendence of winning in business? I think the best thing is to go back to the heading of this section: **Seek prosperity and expect to win.** Do you expect to win? Have you decided that winning is more important than losing or even just blending in? I hope you do because that is what greatness is made of.

You can achieve greatness in life if you put your mind to it and stick to your plan. You can achieve greatness if you stay focused on the end result. You can achieve greatness if believe in yourself. I believe in you…others around believe in you…a loving Almighty God believes in you. Its now time for you to believe in you and for you to reach the pinnacle of success and win!

IX. Avoid Over-Spending and Control Your Costs

In the first few years during his forty year reign, Solomon built a beautiful temple and a spacious palace, he also learned early on to control his costs. By working with his key strategic partners he was able to purchase goods and services at a minimal cost. He utilized the strength of an army of workers that he could afford to pay with minimal wages. Some may feel that he was far too extravagant in his deployment of ornate objects, and maybe we need to consider the fact that "perception is everything" the fact is he did control his costs, and was able to build his empire with minimal out of pocket expense. However, even Solomon eventually broke this rule and had to pay a huge price when he took on too much debt, and somehow forgot about controlling his costs.

One clear example of throwing money away, because it was someone else's money only requires a quick look back in history during the explosion of the dot-com era of the late 1990's.

Many of the dot-com CEO's of the 90's can attest to the foolishness of their ridiculous spending sprees after they received investment capital. The new extravagant buildings, the $8 million Super Bowl ad campaigns, the $200,000 cars, the multi-million dollar homes all were trophies purchased in honor of their newly found capital. The lavish parties and crazy spending practices they threw in honor of their public offerings, which drew them millions in cash, left most of their companies worthless on paper after the crash. These CEO's burned through tens of millions of dollars in the matter of months by hiring far too many people and going on far too many crazy spending sprees. This was all done with the promise of incredible profits for just about any type of product or service sold over the Internet.

Many dot-com executives purchased huge houses, cars, boats, vacation properties, and lavish offices with the investment capital, all in the name of growing a business. I don't believe this was ever expressed or written in their business plans, but because they had money, they figured, "why not spend a little on me...?" These CEO's and many investors fell victim to the over-spending bug and threw their companies into a rapid tailspin.

There were nearly 2,000 dot-com startups launched in the heyday of the of Internet investment frenzy. The memories are still fresh in our minds of mega-failures such as Webvan and eToys, along with the Nasdaq's staggering $4.4 trillion drop in market capitalization over the course of the 30 months. Between its peak in March 2000 and when it reached the bottom of the barrel in September 2002, not only did most of the dot-coms fail, so did many venture capital firms. We now know that the collective business consciousness overreacted to the market potential of the Internet, which led to an inevitable correction.

During this time investors and dot-com CEO's made a very critical error: they somehow forgot to go out and sell something; control their costs; and in turn start turning a profit. It was an ugly time in the history of commerce.

Solomon, unfortunately, also fell victim to extravagance, and in his latter years needed to relinquish property to Hiram in order to pay remaining debts.

In one area Solomon fell short and was no different from many kings of his day, who frequently erected buildings and monuments as symbols of power. Multi-million dollar towers, extravagant casinos, and billion dollar stadiums are erected in honor of the egos of the executives that run the organizations. The temptation to out-due the competition in designing these structures is obviously at the top of the list. But what about paying for these elaborate edifices?

The Dallas Cowboys NFL franchise spent $1.3 billion for their new stadium that opened in 2009. The City of Arlington, TX provided $325 million in funding, and the NFL provided the Cowboys with an additional $150 million, as per their policy for giving teams a certain lump sum of money for stadium finance. Ticket sales, suites and concession sales will be part of the payback package, but what an enormous debt of over $525 million to have to repay. Add in almost $121 million dollars in annual players' salaries to payout, and this ticket is one hefty debt to cover each and every year. To put that into perspective, each fan needs to pay $1,993 per year to cover the costs of the players' salaries, operations, and debt service! So, if I want to go to a game and take two of my children, I would need to invest almost $6,000 annually just to see 8 games!

This is just one example of a disparaging error that leaders make: letting their ego get the best of them by spending extravagantly on buildings and other images. As an athlete, I am a huge sports fan—especially of football, but I don't believe we can keep on paying such huge salaries and over a billion dollars to construct new stadiums and not have some kind of repercussion. Sooner or later the Break-even Analysis doesn't pencil out any longer. Each of us in the world of business must pay careful attention to our costs if we expect to grow.

Think of the millions of dollars spent every year on NFL Super Bowl ads—especially the money spent by many businesses that cannot necessarily afford that extravagant ad campaign on television. For every 30 second commercial during the 2008 Super Bowl, the cost was $2.7 million. Back to our friends during the dot-com fiasco of the nineties, I remember several new dot-com's that paid millions of dollars for Super Bowl advertising, and the Return on Investment was dismal. These companies were no where near to achieving a return on their investment. Sure it brought traffic to their web sites, but they failed to convert customers…paying customers, to the overall mix.

Creating something physically grand, such as a building, especially a gold-lined building, costs an enormous amount of money. How many gold-lined buildings are there in the world today? I would venture a guess that there aren't many. That holds true today as much as in Solomon's day. William Randolph Hearst spent millions building a castle in an era where millions were worth billions in comparison to the dollar's present value. This occurred in the 20th century, and if you take a look at some of the lavish buildings still being constructed, and the homes that newly married couples have built, it makes you wonder if we have learned any lessons along the way.

The lesson we must learn is to make certain that we have the resources to complete our objective. The challenge is to forecast if the economy will still be doing well in five years; or that your team is still winning and bringing in ticket sales (revenue) and sponsors to cover costs; or to predict that oil prices will remain in tact…or a major war will not break out…or a thousand other things.

Stay the course and remain conservative in your spending. High costs mean higher prices, and higher prices result in unhappy customers. *So, it is important to maximize our cash and avoid extravagance or we risk losing property, loyalty, customers, brand equity and other good will.*

X. Exercise Integrity

This might seem irrelevant, as so many "leaders" today break their agreements almost as soon as they are made, but keeping agreements is the #1 key to building goodwill.

Solomon received gifts in exchange for his wisdom. For most of his rule Solomon kept his agreements, and most specifically, his agreement with God, and his wealth became greater than all the kings of the earth. Coincidentally, this is also where Solomon failed. It is detailed in I Kings, how King Solomon loved many foreign women. He erected places of worship in honor of these relationships, many of which were false gods and considered objectionable idols. As a result of his broken vow not to put any idol above God, Solomon then had to deal with many adversaries in the last days of his rule. All of this demise could have been avoided if he would have simply followed his own counsel and kept his oath with God.

The stock market holds companies accountable--for revenue and profitability forecasts. But, even profitable companies can have their stock damaged by simply missing their forecasts. This is because the company forecasts, prior to each earnings release, a report as to how much profit the company expects to make. If the CEO misses the forecast, just watch that stock get hammered on Wall Street. This is because Wall Street cares as much about the company's ability to forecast as it does actual performance. The process is silly and confounding until it happens to your company or a stock in your portfolio, then reality sets in that the rules are set, and they will not be deterred from.

What about the CEO, who promises that the organization will not be going through any reorganization soon; that no offices would be shut down; no lines of business discontinued; and no employees will be let go for at least a period of two years.Four weeks later, you receive a call from a different manager telling you that you are being transferred to a different branch, in a different city because your branch is closing. You are given the option to transfer or seek employment elsewhere.

How eager would you be to work for an organization, or a boss that promises one thing and then delivers something out of left field? You would feel betrayed by the company's senior executives, and it would be next to impossible to ever regain that trust that was broken. Yet, this happens frequently in corporations every day, in every part of the world. If there is one key to building a successful empire, keeping agreements allows us to honor our commitments, and maintain a high level of trust with our colleagues.

In Ecclesiastes, Solomon also takes us through the search for meaning in life from self-indulgent, materialism, and ultimately finding a lack of fulfillment from all of these "meaningless" pursuits. When Solomon looked back upon his personal journey, he acknowledged that his excess consumed him and in the end was "meaningless." Yet, it is here that he recognizes the vanity of so many of his efforts, and comments: *"I know that there is nothing better for them than to rejoice and to do good in one's lifetime; moreover, that every man who eats and drinks sees good in all his labor--it is the gift of God. I know that everything God does will remain forever; there is nothing to add to it and there is nothing to take from it, for God has so worked that men should fear him."* (Ecclesiastes 3:12-14).

The key principle to remember here is that when Solomon kept his agreement with God, he prospered. When he decided he wanted more, and went outside of his covenants to "marry foreign women," his prosperity diminished.

Solomon advises us that there is a time for everything, yet the true meaning for man is to find value and to rejoice in his work. In the book of Ecclesiastes we further learn that there is a time and season for all things. I have always enjoyed the next passage of advice from Solomon because we go through life and at different points and we have different interests, different skills, various levels of motivation, different acquaintances, and even different experiences. Solomon counsels:

XI. Communicate

A leader has to communicate to his/her team in a professional, confident and diplomatic manner on a continuous stream. Even during difficult times we have to face reality by being candid and telling it like it is. It seems like far too many leaders today don't know how to talk straight anymore. Instead, they spend most of their time trying to convince us that things are not really as bad as they seem. It could be denial or it could come down to being dishonest, but if our leader(s) can't or won't clearly communicate what the vision is, it can start to drive you crazy after a while.

Communication has to start with telling the truth, even when it's painful. A leader can't be like the boy who didn't cry wolf when the wolf was at the door. Sooner or later after a prolonged period of time of being told that all is well, even as the economy worsens and more jobs are lost, we stop listening to the bozo's that say all is well.

Communication is the foundation in which we build from. A lack of communication; dishonest or sugar-coated communication with details conveniently left out creates cracks in that foundation, and cracks create weakness. Our empires must be strong and cannot afford any cracks in the foundation.

Earlier we discussed how important clarity is to your empire. Clear, concise, straightforward communication is exactly what every organization needs. I have learned that people will often read something else into what is stated, form their own opinion, change the meaning of what was stated, and completely miss the boat on the message. In many cases the communicator may have missed a word, did not clarify a position, or simply failed to paint a clear picture. When this happens…(notice I said "when" not "if") make certain to restate and clarify and clear up any unclear thoughts or ideas.

On other occasions we have all listened to over-zealous, pompous athletes, celebrities, managers or whomever, and it immediately becomes offensive. First thing to do here is to realize that all they care about is them and their own personal gain. It may come off as confidence, but in reality individuals like this are living in a sad state of insecurity, which is manifest in an over the top fashion to compensate for a lack of attention.

Good leaders will show a balance of professionalism, kindness, confidence, stability, passion, caring, sincerity, candor, accountability and vision in their communication.

I have sat in meetings when the leader addressing the audience exuded all of the above traits, and have heard comments like *"I would follow him anywhere"*, or *"she has the confidence of someone that could lead us out of this mess"*, and *"he is the type of leader that this organization needs to take us to the next level."* **Effective leaders have mastered the art of communication and are capable of gathering buy-in and solidarity.**

We would all do well to master this art form and use it to build our empires.

XII. Exercise Common Sense

Throughout most of his rule, Solomon exercised common sense in a fashion that became methodical. When he penned over 3,000 proverbs it was clear that he had learned many important principles of thinking things through clearly prior to acting. His wisdom that he showed forth was also a common sense approach to finding a solution to a problem. Whether it was two mothers in a quarrel; strategic alliances that needed to be formed; enemies turned into alliances; establishing key trade routes; or building a beautiful edifice to God, Solomon exercised common sense during most of his reign. It wasn't until his latter days as king when he allowed himself to get caught up in the thought process of "look at me and how great I am," that he started to falter.

One clear lesson to learn from Solomon and thousands of other leaders throughout the millennia, is that you can't be an effective leader if you don't have Common Sense. Period. This is a basic principle of leadership that sadly eludes many otherwise talented leaders. Leaders are made, not born. Leadership is forged in times of crisis. It's easy to sit there with your feet up on the desk and talk theory, or tell other how to run things, or even to instruct students how to start and run a business when you've never been on the business battlefield yourself.

When I was in college I was taught by professors with MBA's and PhD's that couldn't figure out how to unlock the front door of a small business, let alone run one. They taught us on theory that a small business is like managing a group of students. It's not, never was. Managing students doesn't require *Passion* to get you up at 4:00 am and keep you working until midnight day in and day out, on a problem that requires a solution – or your entire business could be in jeopardy.

Running a business *Does* require ingenuity, passion, marketing street smarts, innovation, finance/funding and a competent management team that exercises common sense for the good of the enterprise, and about 3,000 other things that we don't have room to go into.

It's another thing to lead when your world comes tumbling down and you need to figure out a positive outcome right now because your 140 employees and your banker are depending on you to solve the problem. Theory doesn't teach that.

Remember that the only thing you've got going for you as a human being is your ability to reason and exercise common sense in times of crises. If you don't know a dip of cow manure from a dip of vanilla ice cream, you'll never make it as a leader. (More about Common Sense in Chapter 7).

In the end, Solomon reflected upon his worldly success and came to a conclusion for all of us to find the true meaning of a successful life:

- fear God at all times,

- seek wisdom, and

- enjoy our days while we are still here to enjoy them.

Solomon advised us to stand in awe of God: *"When you make a vow to God, do not delay in fulfilling it. He has no pleasure in fools; fulfill your vow."* Yes, keeping our agreements matters very, very much, and exercising common sense is as important.

> **From the Source**
>
> *"When you make a vow to God, do not delay in fulfilling it. He has no pleasure in fools; fulfill your vow."*
>
> **- Solomon**

Thus, there you have the 12 keys to building a successful empire. To summarize, they are as follows:

12 Key Principles to Building a Successful Empire

I. **Seek Wisdom** – Seek wisdom from God and find success

II. **Provide Clarity** – Choose clarity over certainty

III. **Develop Strategic Alliances** – Keep focused on adding strategic allies you can count on

IV. **Look for Opportunities** – Always look for opportunities to expand your areas of trade

V. **Stay Focused** – Amid all of the clutter, empires that focus on their primary mission achieve success

VI. **Purge Conflicts and Train Your Leaders** – Train your leaders to be loyal to the building up of the empire

VII. **Hold Others Accountable** – Seek accountability over being popular

VIII. **Seek Prosperity and Expect to Win** – Raise your sights for greater accomplishments. Think success; live success; and work for success.

IX. **Avoid Over Spending and Control Costs** – Spend what you need to achieve objectives, but avoid lavish lifestyles

X. **Exercise Integrity** – Broken agreements lead to the demise of the empire

XI. **Communicate** – Use straight talk and clearly communicate the vision

XII. **Exercise Common Sense** – Effective leaders always incorporate common sense

CHAPTER THREE

Solomon's Kingdom

*"It requires wisdom to understand wisdom: the
music is nothing if the audience is deaf."*
                                          – Walter Lippmann

Solomon's wisdom was based on a humble request to God about being able to fairly judge His people: *"Give therefore thy servant an understanding heart to judge they people, that I may discern between good and bad; for who is able to judge this thy so great a people?"*

Solomon's wish was granted because his *"speech pleased the Lord, that Solomon had asked this thing."* His appeal did not include a selfish desire to be made wealthy; or to have his enemies destroyed. He simply asked for *understanding to discern judgment.*

Solomon became ruler of Israel in approximately 1015, and his kingdom extended from the Euphrates River in the north to Egypt in the south.

The name Solomon, in Hebrew is *Shlomo* and translates to "peaceful," "complete" or "prosperous," from the Hebrew *shalom.* The name given by God to Solomon in the Bible is Jedidiah,

---

Definition

The name Solomon, in Hebrew is *Shlomo* and translates to "peaceful," "complete" or "prosperous," from the Hebrew *shalom.* The name given by God to Solomon in the Bible is Jedidiah, meaning "friend of God" or, more precisely "beloved of Yah" (variant form of "Yahweh"), (2 Samuel 12:25), and some scholars have speculated that Solomon is a "dragon name" taken either when he assumed the throne or upon his death.

---

meaning "friend of God" or, more precisely "beloved of Yah" (variant form of "Yahweh"), (2 Samuel 12:25), and some scholars have speculated that Solomon is a "dragon name" taken either when he assumed the throne or upon his death.

Solomon's birth was considered a grace from God, after the death of the previous child between David and Bathsheba. Those who are named Solomon in modern society are considered *"men amongst boys."* They are considered natural born leaders, especially in the Ethiopian community, and are generally thought to be very wise.

Solomon was David's thirtieth son. Solomon's mother was Bathsheba. According to the Biblical account, David passed over his oldest living son, Adonijah, and instead declared Solomon heir to the throne. When Adonijah tried to seize the throne as most jealous older brothers would try to do, Bathsheba and Nathan appealed to David, who immediately had Solomon crowned king.

Many scholars believe that Solomon was the author and majority contributor to the book of Proverbs in the Old Testament. But it is also clear that there are a few additional authors which contributed to the book, such as "the wise" (22:17); Agur (30:1); and King Lemuel (31:1).

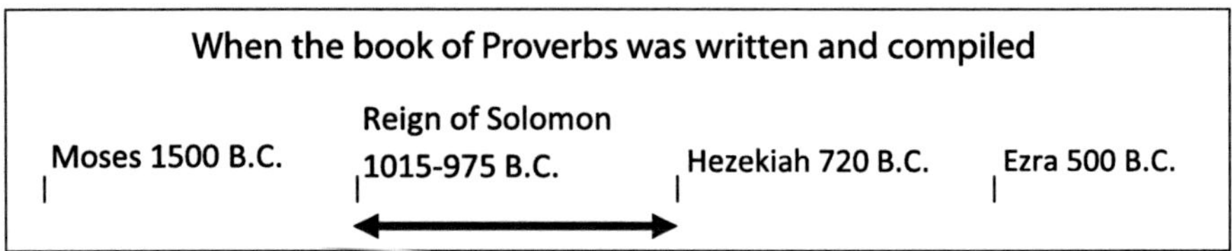

Just as the quote at the beginning of this chapter illustrates, the music is not heard if the audience turns a deaf ear to what is being offered. Is it up to us to figure out if others teachings are wise? Or, is it up to each of us to exercise prudence and wisdom as we face decisions? I believe it is both questions that we must consider in all walks of life.

We each play a role in becoming that "audience" waiting to be instructed, hoping to be enlightened, or even possibly entertained. We are all part of the "audience" when it comes to listening to the music of life. Some enjoy Country over Rock, others choose Rap over Classical (not sure why…!), but you get the idea.

The "audience" is made up of those that are willing and able to be entertained, advised, and instructed. We are the audience to learn from Solomon. And, not just Solomon but all who provide some type of wisdom for us to follow.

I think back of my days in growing up with my wonderful parents and how they taught my sisters and me to be good citizens, and God-fearing people who respects others, and hold a tender reverence for the freedoms that we enjoy living in the United States of America, and any other free country.

Most everyone has been a participant in an audience in one form or another. The members of the audience, or congregation, expect to be educated and instructed to make their lives better and to form a bond of some kind.

At work we perform our duties to the best of our ability (at least I hope you do), and to be fairly compensated for the work that we offer. For some, compensation is the only reason they work; for others they work because they enjoy it; and yet for even others, they work to make a difference.

Maybe a brief explanation of what the responsibilities are of an audience might be helpful. The following list of duties of an audience might be enlightening in helping us to determine how we can become an active audience to the wise teachings of an inspired king.

Arrive – you have to be present in some form to participate.

Listen and Show Respect – the presenter of information or entertainment should be given proper respect to allow them to get their message out.

Respond (with satisfaction or dissatisfaction) – showing approval or disapproval lets the presenter know that you have acknowl-edged their performance.

Learn – no matter how good or bad the presentation is, we can always learn something.

Take Action – we can take action in several ways: discussing with others what we heard or saw; purchasing products; singing along; and most importantly-put into practice what we learn;

Depart – sooner or later you have to move on and leave the scene of participation.

The audience in Solomon's day was vast. The kingdom of Israel achieved its greatest glory during the reign of King Solomon. Solomon's kingdom also controlled a vast region east of the river in what is today the Kingdom of Jordan, and deep into the northeast, reaching far beyond the Golan Heights all the way to the Euphrates

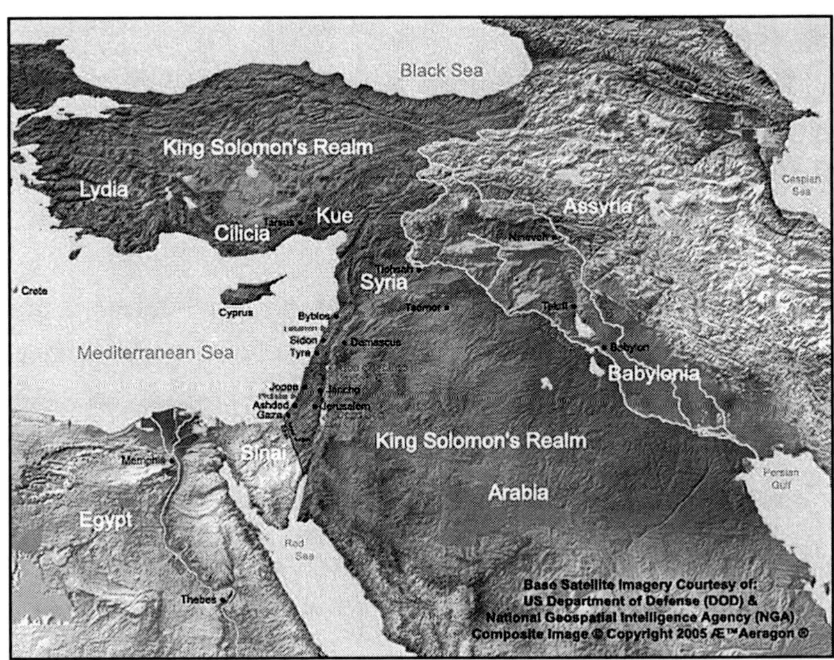

River. It was most certainly a very different Middle East than today.

Under Solomon's leadership and wisdom, he developed an empire that not only was vast in geography, it was powerful in trade as well as military prowess. Solomon was a master at developing a plan of action and then executing the plan. His plan was simple, yet brilliant if you take into account how he kept his enemies at bay by forming strategic alliances. The further brilliance of his plan also instilled in their minds that the House of David ruled by divine will. Today we can't necessarily instill in the minds of our competitors that we rule by divine influence, but forming strategic alliances should be at the top of any game plan.

Solomon also built fortified towns in the surrounding areas of Jerusalem--Megiddo, Hazor, Gezer, Beth-Horon. He established new cities and towns for his army to reinforce the protection that his army could provide in a close-knit manner. These fortified cities were developed with innovative water conduits that provided necessary nourishment to a parched region. This elaborate watering system also allowed the cities to withstand advances from opposing forces.

Solomon built an empire that was not only *impressive*, it was just as *oppressive* to rebel forces, shutting them down from gaining access to key cities. His kingdom was a centralized monarchy that was an empire to be admired and admonished.

Throughout Israel, Solomon fortified the great cities: "And this is the reason for the labor force which King Solomon raised: to build the house of the LORD, his own house, the Millo, the wall of Jerusalem, Hazor, Megiddo, and Gezer" (I Kings 9:15).

Regarding Jerusalem, as long as the Temple Mount is disputed between Arabs and Jews, no excavations are permitted in the immediate area where Solomon's temple once stood. Wouldn't it be great though if we could actually get a glimpse into the archeological digs that are buried beneath the Temple Mount.

Solomon expanded and fortified other cities but is there any archaeological evidence that supports the biblical records? The answer is yes, and thanks to archeologists in the past century, we now have evidence of the elaborate system of strategic cities that Solomon built to fortify his empire.

The first city mentioned is Hazor, a northern Israelite territory that was lost in time until last century. The first extensive excavations were done under the direction of archaeologist Yigael Yadin in the 1950's. Yadin writes about Hazor, "What I'm about to say may sound like something out of a detective story, but it's true. Our great guide was the Bible. As an archaeologist, I can't imagine anything more exciting than to work with the Bible in one hand and a spade in the other. This was the real secret of our discovery of the Solomonic period" (*Hazor*, Random House, New York, 1975).

Yadin found the elaborate and sturdy main gate and part of the wall of the city, which archaeologists now call the *Solomonic style of architecture*. Eventually, he found the same "Solomonic-type" gate in all three of the cities mentioned in the Bible.

In the most recent excavation of Megiddo in 1993, archaeologists Israel Finkelstein and David Ussishkin report, "The grandeur of Solomon's Megiddo is clearly evident in the archaeological finds at Megiddo-in large palaces, with fine, smooth-faced ashlar masonry and in elaborate decorative stonework" ("Back to Megiddo," *Biblical Archaeology Review*, January/February 1994, p. 36).

The further portion of the Solomon's plan explains that his empire was divided into twelve districts, which were symbolic to the 12 sons of Jacob. Eleven of these districts paid regularly tribute to Solomon. The tribe of Judah was apparently exempted from this tax, and this allowed Solomon to strengthen his hold over his own tribe. However, this also deepened the tension between Judah and the other tribes and the tension would eventually become too disruptive after Solomon's death. During the reign of his son Rehoboam, this tension proved to be insurmountable, and war soon broke out.

King Solomon's reign also enjoyed the fruits of his commercial and political ties with neighboring kingdoms. As was pointed out in Chapter Two, developing strategic alliances is key to building an empire. Solomon entered into an alliance with Hiram, King of Tyre, who provided him with cedar wood for building the Temple. Solomon also built up an alliance with the Egyptian pharaoh (presumably Siamun of the twenty-first dynasty), who gave his daughter as wife to Solomon. This alliance also provided him ownership of the town of Gezer as part of his new wife's dowry.

During his reign, Solomon did not have foreign enemies to threaten his empire and he also found a powerful ally in King Hiram, who was a faithful friend of his father, David.

"Now Hiram king of Tyre sent his servants to Solomon, because he heard that they had anointed him king in place of his father, for Hiram had always loved David . . . So the LORD gave Solomon wisdom, as He had promised him; and there was peace between Hiram and Solomon, and the two of them made a treaty together" (1Kings 5:1,12).

Alliances with foreign royal families brought together through marriage, together with political treaties and commercial relations, provided additional recognition and placed more importance on Jerusalem and is evidenced by the famous visit of the Queen of Sheba (1 Kings, 10).

Solomon was a progressive ruler. He possessed a skill for taking advantage of foreign knowledge and foreign skills and turning them to his own advantage. That was the secret, otherwise scarcely understandable, of how the nation. . . developed quickly into an economic unstoppable force. This was also the secret of his wealth, which the

Bible emphasizes. Solomon imported smelting technicians from Phoenicia. Hiram . . . , a craftsman from Tyre, was entrusted with the casting of the Temple furnishings (1 Kings 7:13,14).

The Phoenicians had practical experience that was accumulated over many centuries. In the area that the Phoenicians inhabited know as Ezion-Geber, Solomon founded an important enterprise for over-seas trade . . . Solomon therefore sent to Tyre for specialists for his dockyards and sailors for his ships: 'And Hiram sent in the navy his servants, shipmen that had knowledge of the sea . . .' (1Kings 9:27)" (Werner Keller, *The Bible As History*, Bantam, New York, 1980, pp. 211-212. On Ezion-Geber, see Gary D. Pratico, "Where Is Ezion-Geber?", *Biblical Archaeology Review*, September/October 1986, pp. 24-35; Alexander Flinder, "Is This Solomon's Seaport?", *Biblical Archaeology Review*, July/August 1989, pp. 31-42).

The account of the Queen of Sheba

I'm not quite sure why, but one of the more unusual accounts about Solomon is consigned to myth by some scholars. It concerns the visit of the queen of Sheba.

> *"Now when the queen of Sheba heard of the fame of Solomon concerning the name of the LORD, she came to test him with hard questions. She came to Jerusalem with a very great retinue, with camels that bore spices, very much gold, and precious stones; and when she came to Solomon, she spoke with him about all that was in her heart. So Solomon answered all her questions; there was nothing so difficult for the king that he could not explain it to her .*
>
> *"Then she said to the king: "It was a true report which I heard in my own land about your words and your wisdom. However I did not believe the words until I came and saw with my own eyes; and indeed the half was not told me.*

(1Kings 10:1-10).

This story has been the inspiration for many paintings and movies, but does it have historical backing? Where was the kingdom of Sheba? Until the 20th Century, the sands of time very probably covered up much of this great kingdom of the past.

Yet it was well known by some of the classical Greek and Roman writers. "In happy Arabia," wrote Dionysius the Greek in A.D. 90, *"you can always smell the sweet perfume of marvelous spices, wheth-er it be incense or wonderful myrrh. Its inhabitants have great flocks of sheep in the meadows, and birds fly in from distant isles bringing leaves of pure cinnamon."*

Another Greek historian, Diodorus (100 B.C.), writes: *"These people surpass in riches and luxuries not only their Arab neighbors, but also the rest of the world. They drink out of cups made of gold and silver . . . The Sabeans enjoy this luxury because they are convinced that riches which come from the earth are the favor of the gods and should be shown to others."*

The Roman Emperor Augustus actually sent an army of 10,000 men to southern Arabia to plunder this wealth. But the withering desert and frequent plagues decimated the army before they could arrive in the capital. They never fulfilled their mission.

Scholars generally agree that the kingdom of Sheba is located in the southern end of the Arabian Peninsula, now called Yemen. The area is quite isolated and desolate now, but this has not always been the

58

case. "The most prominent of the Arab states . . . during the first half of the 1st millennium B.C.," comments The New Bible Dictionary, "Sheba was ruled by mukarribs, priest-kings, who supervised both the political affairs and the polytheistic worship of the sun, moon and star gods. Explorations (in 1950-1953) . . . found some outstanding examples of Sabean art and architecture, especially the temple of the moon-god at Marib, the capital, which dates from the 7th century B.C. . . ." (The New Bible Dictionary p. 1087).

Until the 20th century, this area of Yemen was largely off-limits to archaeologists. Now, up to 4,000 inscriptions of this ancient kingdom have come to light, confirming that one of the four nations in the area was called Sheba and that the population of at least one of its cities totaled a million inhabitants.

It is suggested that this part of the world was not always dry and barren. It once had abundant water to irrigate the precious spice crops. The two most popular spices grown were frankincense (a resin of incense) and myrrh. The fragrant perfume of frankincense was used in temples and homes of the rich to ask favors from the gods. Myrrh was an indispensable oil used as a beauty aid to keep the skin smooth and soft, and was also used to embalm the dead. The Magi gave these two valuable spices to the infant Jesus as gifts fit for a newborn king (Matthew 2:11).

Frankincense and *Myrrh* are also symbols of royalty and were given as gifts in ancient times. The account of the birth of Jesus and the three wise men to see that these three kings truly believed they were paying their respects to a future king.

The evidence of abundant water in Sheba comes from the remains of a huge dam found in the area, and explains how it could be called "Happy Arabia" by the ancients. Yemen is the origin land of all Arabs in the Middle East. In ancient times, Yemen was an important center of trade and power. Many powerful kingdoms were in Yemen, including the Sabaeans. Yemen was important in the trade of spices as well.

It was known to the ancient Romans as *Arabia Felix* ("Happy Arabia" in Latin). They called it Happy Arabia because the area was so beautiful and powerful. (Source: Wikipedia, 2008)

A gigantic dam blocked the river Adhanat in Sheba collecting the rainfall from a wide area. The water was then led off in canals for irrigation purposes, which was what gave the land its fertility. Remains of this technical marvel in the shape of walls over 60 feet high still defy the sand-dunes of the desert. Just as Holland is in modern times the Land of Tulips, so Sheba was then the Land of Spices, one vast scented garden of the costliest spices in the world.

There is yet much to explore in this area of ancient Sheba, and it is still a dangerous place to go due to a lack of water, but much scientific progress has been made. What the famed archaeologist W.F. Albright remarked about these excavations in 1953 still holds true: "They are in process of revolutionizing our knowledge of Southern Arabia's cultural history and chronology. Up to now the results to hand demonstrate the political and cultural primacy of Sheba in the first centuries after 1000 B.C."

As time goes by, more archaeological evidence continues to indicate that Solomon's reign was actually as magnificent as the Bible resolutely records. This area of Sheba was indeed a strategic path for Solomon's armies and trade routes to travel through. ***Once again signifying that his brilliance was in planning a strategy and executing the plan.***

The Wisdom in the Layout of Solomon's Temple

We should spend a few moments discussing the wisdom of the layout of Solomon's Temple. The original Temple of God in Jerusalem was constructed during the reign of King Solomon. Although far greater in size and magnificence, the structure was similar in layout to the small, portable Tabernacle in the Wilderness that it replaced.

The temple took 7 years to construct, and Solomon's Temple had a life of a little over 360 years, from about 950 to 586 B.C. when it was looted and burned by the Babylonians.

Solomon's Temple (also known as the First Temple) was, according to the Torah and the Bible, the first Jewish temple in Jerusalem. It functioned as a religious focal point for worship and the sacrifices known as the "korbanot" in ancient Judaism. The temple was destroyed by the Babylonians in 586 BCE.

There are a few areas of the temple that should be pointed out which represent the wisdom of Solomon, and the inspiration given to Solomon in constructing the magnificent temple in God's honor.

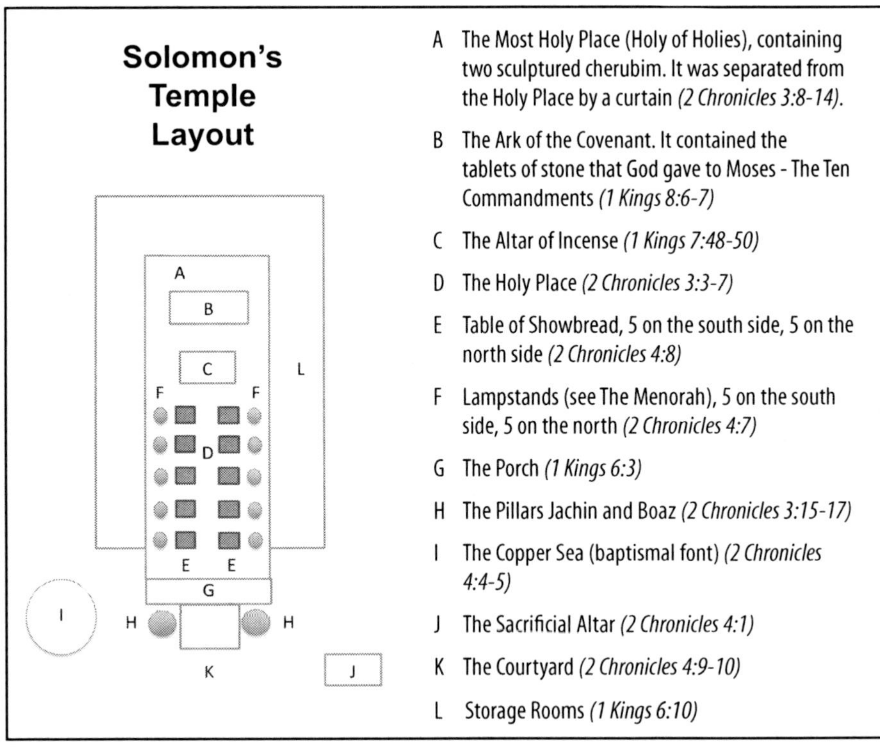

Scholars have tried over the centuries to depict what the temple actually looked like. Most all of them agree that the Temple was a rectangular building with a simple, yet efficient design for maneuverability.

They agree on a few main points such as the main entrance was located on the east side of the structure with cells on the north, south and west sides for the priests to store precious items. The Holy of Holies housed the Ark of the Covenant, and it contained the tablets of stone that God gave to Moses, or what we know of today as the Ten Commandments.

The pillars at the entrance of the temple (one on the north and one on the south) were symbols of leaders familiar to Solomon: Jachin and Boaz. The names denote "He will establish" and "In him is strength."

Just outside of the temple entrance stood the baptismal font upheld by 12 oxen. Three oxen faced north; three faced east, three faced west and three faced south, and the font was situated on the backs of the oxen.

When a structure lasts almost 400 years, the wisdom in building such an edifice must have come from someone who was very prudent, or from someone who was truly inspired to build such a structure – or both.

So, the question we need to ask ourselves is: ***How do you and I build empires and processes in our day-to-day operations that will withstand the onslaught of destructive forces?*** Conventional wisdom would tell us to:

- create a blueprint;

- follow each and every step of the blueprint;

- develop a plan of action and follow the plan;

- update the plan when necessary;

- report our progress to stakeholders;

- execute the plan and make changes, or corrections when needed;

- upon completion, or achievement of success, give credit where credit is due.

I hope you are interested in following this type of wisdom, because if you are, you stand a very high chance of being successful in just about anything you set out to do.

It is up to us to figure out the action plan and execute on a sustainable system.

CHAPTER FOUR

Making a Profound Impression

*"I don't think much of a man who is not wiser
today than he was yesterday."*

– Abraham Lincoln

Let's take a journey and look at a few verses from Proverbs. My goal here is to point out that we have a few pearl in our hands…a diamond in the ruff…a true gem to behold. The commentary that you will find at the end of each chosen verse is my own interpretation of how Solomon's wisdom may assist us today in the further development of our society.

Does Solomon's wisdom apply today as it did over 3,000 years ago? The simple answer is yes, and probably more so, because the world is very different and we need wisdom to help us become a more cohesive society.

When I was sitting in Church listening to a group discussion about a few select verses from Proverbs, I felt like Solomon was speaking to me directly. The first verse that we covered was found in Proverbs 3:5-6: *Trust in the LORD with all thine heart; and lean not unto thine own understanding. In all thy ways acknowledge him, and he shall direct thy paths.*

I had read these words many times in my life and they have helped me earlier during some trying times.

The lesson continued with the next verse found in Chapter 1 Verse 10: *My son if sinners entice thee, consent thou not.* This made me reflect on the lesson's I had learned in business over the past two decades, and the not-so-honorable business partners and associates I had done business with over the years. That verse seemed to fit as well in my life.

The next verse that we covered as a congregation was Chapter 12 verses 11-12: *He that tilleth his land shall be satisfied with bread: but he that followeth vain persons is void of understanding. The wicked desireth the net of evil men: but the root of the righteous yieldeth fruit.*

This one, and the following 6 discussions about certain topics all had a parallel meaning in my life in one fashion or another, and they made a profound impression on me. It was at that point that I realized that I had to dive into the Wisdom of Solomon and figure out if the meanings 3,000 years ago were of any value to us today…3,000 years later…in a different part of the world…with much different ways of life.

Could these verses be universal enough to transcend time, cultures, religions, societies, etc.? I strongly believe the answer is YES! And we should do whatever we can to learn from the richest, most wise king of his day in the entire world.

Could it come down to something as simple as asking God to grant Solomon's request? This is the beginning, and then Solomon had to get to work and make things happen. He was a man of action, and had a strong desire to help others, and to be successful in his endeavors. At the same time he was blessed with the riches of the world, and the respect of many. I think this is a fascinating discussion, and I really wanted to find out more about this king.

Take for example, one Proverb that is simple, yet powerful to the wise student who will listen to this counsel: *"Trust in the Lord with all thine heart and lean not unto thine own understanding. In all thy ways acknowledge him, and he shall direct thy paths" (Proverbs 3:5).* Many times in this life we are called to walk by faith, in business and in our personal lives, and expected to rely upon God's power and mercy. But I will be the first to admit that this is not always the case.

So, let's take a closer look at what he wrote and begin to dissect some of the meanings of the verses as they were written.

The book of Proverbs teaches us about human behavior and social conduct, as well as spiritual values that can be used every day of our lives. The book can be summarized under the following categories:

1. Seek True Wisdom

2. Welcome Good Advice

3. Steer Clear of Corrupt Friends

4. Help Those in Need

5. Avoid Improper Speech

6. Enjoy Hard Work

1. **Seek True Wisdom** – Proverbs stresses the point of seeking wisdom: (1: 1-7; 2:1-9; 3:1-12; 4:1-13; 18:15; 22:17-21; 28:4-9). Wisdom is imparted liberally to those who ask for it believingly (See James 1:5). Seeking true wisdom means that you ask God to grant you wisdom, for He is the source of all knowledge. Why wouldn't we want to go to the source of all knowledge to learn as much as we possibly can?

2. **Welcome Good Advice** – The wise person recognizes that true wisdom comes from God, and we should value the advice of trustworthy, good friends. We should also ignore the bad advice we receive from those who are not concerned about our highest moral welfare. This is a favorite theme in Proverbs, and excellent advice: that children should take the advice of parents 1:8-9; 6: 20-22; and the theme is expounded in various ways 9:7-12; 10:8, 17; 12:1; 13:1, 18; 15:32-33; 19:20; 21:11; 23:12-25; 28:23; 29:17-18. You will see from these passages that the wise person does not take well to people who will not listen when they are in error or danger.

3. **Steer clear of Corrupt Friends** – I think we all we would agree that bad companionships and alliances lead to bad decisions and tainted behavior. Several verses read like the advice of a loving father to his son before he goes up to the wicked city. 1:10-19; 2:12-22; 4:14-19; 5:1-23; 6:23-29; 7:1-27; 9:13-18. Similar themes are revealed around the "bad friends" concept in 13:20; 22:24; 23:6-8, 26-35; 28:10-18; 29:3.

4. **Help Those in Need** – There is more to life than always worrying about ourselves. There are millions of needy people in all parts of the world, even in our own communities. Ours is the responsibility to reach out and lend a hand. A few verses teach this important principle: 3:27-35; 14:21-22, 31; 19:17; 21:13; 22:9; 28:27; 29:7.

5. **Avoid Improper Speech** – Speaking in a tone and manner becoming a leader is forever a good idea. Proverbs deals with community life and personal life. We have witnessed over the centuries that much unhappiness in communities is caused by careless talk. Much strife and unnecessary angst has come as a result of gossip, backbiting, and outright lies. We are counseled to use proper speech and avoid the pitfalls of deceitful talk: 4:20-27; 6:1-5;

   Solomon spends quite a bit of time telling us to watch our speech: 6:12-19; 10:11-14, 18-21, 31-32; 11:9-14; 12:17-23; 13:3; 14:3-7, 25; 15: 1-7, 23, 26; 16:10, 13; 21:21, 27-33; 17:7, 20, 27-28; 18:1-8; 19:1, 5, 27-29; 20:15-20; 21:6, 9, 19, 23-24; 22:10-11; 24:28-29; 25: 8-28. Also there are a few extra passages that deal with both good and bad speech: 26:17-28; 27:1-6; 29:5.

6. **Enjoy Hard Work** – An honest day's work for an honest day's pay has been excellent advice for a long time. It is a privilege to be able to work and to earn a living. Just ask those who are or have been unemployed while the bills are piling up. Do we bring our A-game to work every day? If not we should change our attitude or change our job. Plenty of advice here as well: 10:4-5, 16, 26;

13:4, 11; 189; 19:24; 20:4, 13; 21:17, 25-26; 22:13; 24:27, 30-34.

The next step is to highlight a few of the Proverbs that offer wise counsel to us all. In this next section you will notice that I have taken the liberty to discuss some of the verses in a little more detail and to expound on the meaning of the verse. These are my own interpretations and one man's opinion of what Solomon was trying to teach us.

Proverbs Chapter 1

Verse 3: *To receive the instruction of wisdom, justice and judgment, and equity.*

The beginning of the verses that we will study in this section starts us off with good advice. This is an interesting concept: wisdom… justice… judgment…and equity all in one nice, tight little package. Can these four concepts exist together? Maybe they don't need to. Did both women view Solomon as being wise? Did they both view the judgment was equitable for both of them? The answer is no.

I do believe that we are constantly learning and that each of us must seek out mentors to help us along the way. There is certainly wisdom in being just and fare and equitable with others without passing poor judgment on them. If you are unable to choose a mentor that you know in your circle of influence, then choose a mentor that can teach you through other means…books, the Internet, the news, their example, and so forth.

Verse 5: *A man will hear, and will increase learning; and a man of understanding shall attain unto wise counsels.*

As we hear things that we did not know-or that we hear for the first time, we file this new-found knowledge away and our brain puts it into an area that we can recall again sometime. This also allows us to continue to increase what we know and develop a more sure foundation of knowledge.

I have been very fortunate to have learned many valuable principles from my good parents. After going through several years of thinking I had the world by the tail, and that I knew it all, *I* realized that I didn't, and that my parents did. They knew me better than I knew myself, but they gave me counsel and guidance, and allowed me to make a choice of how I would act. Today as parents, my wife and I go to my parents and my in-laws and ask them what to do in certain situations in raising our children.

Our challenge is to not only continue learning, but to apply what we learn, and to seek out those that are wiser than us. As we seek out advice from others that have obtained wisdom, a light comes on and illuminates the situation even brighter.

As you enter an unfamiliar, darkened room at night the first thing you seek to do is seek to illuminate the room with light to see your way around. Finding our way around a problem can be very similar… at first you seek to find that light as quickly as possible in order to move to your next task.

So what about this "man of understanding", and why should he/we "attain unto wise counsels"? When does someone become one who has understanding? That mostly comes from experience and having been faced with many opportunities to make choices. We should all strive to seek out opportunities to make decisions, and take on tough assignments…it helps us learn and grow.

Verse 7: *The fear of the Lord is the beginning of knowledge: but fools despise wisdom and instruction.*

This one is fairly easy to understand, and at the same time difficult to express, but we should discuss it in some fashion. Knowledge comes from the origin of our own existence.

God has wisdom and knowledge far greater than we can comprehend. As Solomon points out, we must have a fear of God, or in other words, believe that we can receive blessings from Him when we do what is right, we "fear" not receiving those blessings. So if this "fear" is the beginning of knowledge where do we go from there?

The second part of this verse begins to explain it: *but fools despise wisdom and instruction.* Solomon provides us with instruction and wisdom that there is a God and He is here to bless us. He further exudes that we must trust in the Lord and seek out His blessings.

Verse 10: *My son if sinners entice thee, consent thou not.*

Do you believe in right and wrong; good and evil; virtue and vice? Assuming that you do, a simple way of getting to the bottom of the real meaning of this passage is to realize that people do stupid things, and in order to feel a part of the crowd, we go along with the same path.

It reminds me of the time my father told me to "be good" when I went out with some of my friends in school. He knew that a few friends of the group were not the best influences and that they had a pretence to do stupid things as teenage boys will do. There were twelve of us that were headed to one of the friends house to watch the Bears play the Packers on Monday Night Football. When we arrived one of the friends announced that he had a porno film and beer, and his parents were out of town. If anyone wanted to go to his house there would be a party that "we wouldn't forget" and that the football game would be lame.

Six of us said we would stay and watch the game, while the other six decided to go off for a little adventure. The long and short of this story is that those of us that stayed to watch game had a great time, and we stayed out of trouble.

The next day we found out that my friends parents had come home early (probably parents intuition), and they found their son and the other five friends, drunk, horny, and out of control.

Think of the embarrassment and the consequences! I'm sure the parents would love to forget the image of these good boys in a cir-cumstance that was not at all what they felt these boys would participate in. My friends were all grounded and the embarrassment they caused their families was not at all worth the price they had to pay for a little pleasure.

So, how does this relate to business? It taught me a valuable lesson: to always to listen to my Dad and not allow friends and associates to persuade me to do things I should not participate in, or that went against my values.

I think we all would agree that we have been approached in some fashion to do things that were not on the up and up. Maybe it was to show sales that did not exist to pump up a stock price. Maybe it was to take credit for something that we did not do. Maybe it was to steal confidential information for our own gain. Whatever it was, or may be someday, the caution is not to yield to the temptation of doing something you will regret. ***Do not give in, and do not give your consent to allow someone else to persuade you to do something improper.***

Verse 14: *Cast in thy lot among us; let us have one purse.*

This verse is calling out to its readers: "Come with us and we will build a team, and with teamwork we stand a far greater chance of being successful!" I could write volumes about teamwork and the special bond that exists with the players and participants of a winning team. But let it suffice to say that in business TEAMWORK is sometimes as important as market trends and growth. When you consider achieving the highest success possible and working together to do so, the word TEAM sums it up with one simple acronym:

Together

Everyone

Achieves

More

When everyone achieves more as they work together to reach a common goal, it is a good thing. As we work together to achieve that goal, a stronger bond is formed, and at some point nothing can stand in the way of success. Our job is to figure out who the team is, what the goal is, and how we will work together to achieve it. A sports team; a family team, a work team, a social team…it does not matter what the team is, what matters is that everyone is on the same page of the game plan, and the plan moves forward with each individual taking on a specific role.

What is your role on the team? I can pretty much guarantee that your role is important to the overall success of the team, and that others are depending on you.

When I became injured with severe head injuries in football, my role changed from being the star on the field to being the supporter on the sidelines. When we won the National Championship in college football, my teammates expected me to lift them up and tell them how good they were; pointing out their mistakes; and generally supporting them.

Two decades later, I still wear my National Championship ring just like Robbie Bosco, the MVP of the title game (BYU vs Michigan 1984) does. We all had a role to play, however important as on the front lines, or however mundane as cheering on my teammates, or playing a service role on the sidelines offering praise, pointing out errors, coaching, etc. Everyone was important to the overall outcome…winning the National title.

Verses 17-19: *Surely in vain the net is spread in the sight of any bird. And they lay wait for their own blood; they lurk privily for their own lives. So are the ways of every one that is greedy of gain; which taketh away the life of the owners thereof.*

How many times have you and I read about the greed that others

Key Point

As we work together to achieve that goal, a stronger bond is formed, and at some point nothing can stand in the way of success.

possess, and how people have suffered by the hand of one, or at least the minority? The fact is we see this all too often today in business we see it, we hear it and read about this ugly characteristic of human beings. When did they turn this way? Did they happen to be born greedy? Is there no way of controlling greed?

The sad part of this verse is that those who are in this life to get personal gain, can actually suck out the life of those they harm. Maybe not right then and there, but certainly down the road due to the stress they can cause. And, yes in some sad cases the life was literally sucked out immediately due to taking a life in murder or suicide. It is a repulsive topic to discuss, but it is also a topic that deserves our attention.

Greed by its very nature is harmful in so many facets. Greed is a selfish and excessive desire for more of something (as money) than is needed. No one trusts someone who is greedy since the game is too exhaustive waiting for them to "strike" and cast their snare. So much time and energy, and money is usually lost trying to acquire more.

Verses 24-25: *Because I have called and ye refused; I have stretched out my hand and no man regarded; but ye have set at naught all my counsel, and would not of my reproof.*

Speaking as a parent and as a boss, to set at naught my counsel when it is given is not only frustrating it is annoying. I realize I am not the wisest person on the planet, but I believe I speak for most parents and bosses, we do know a few things that we have learned through experience.

The counsel rendered by wise leaders, can be an invaluable tool to have access to and to apply in our lives. As a child we hopefully listened to our parents not to touch the hot stove. As a teenager we hopefully listened to our teachers to take good notes and listen to the lectures in order to do well on the exam. As young adults we hope-fully listened to our parents to choose good friends. Early on in our working careers we hopefully listened to the wisdom of a boss that reminded us to be on time and render good customer service. As a business owner or manager we hopefully have listened to seasoned mentors that shed a little light on how to maneuver through the maze of running a small business.

Have you ever had someone offer a hand of friendship, or a word of advice that was timely? Timely in the sense that it was probably something you needed to hear at that particular moment, or you needed a friend to help you out in a time of crisis or concern. Yet then we came to that fork in the road…to take the advice and heed it, or discard it and send it off to oblivion never to be thought of again.

I once had a discussion with a wealthy individual who had acquired great wealth in the insurance business. He was highly focused on seeing the mark he wanted to achieve, and then nothing stood in his way to accomplish his mission. His "mission" was to close as many deals as possible, as quickly as possible, with as little expense as possible. He was/is a very Red, A-type personality who is very driven. But he was focused. His focus was so relentless that he had the worlds best blinders on most of the time to stay focused on his goal. Once the goal was achieved he was ready to move on to the next challenge and begin the process all over again.

My purpose in telling you this is not to make you feel like you and I need to be so relentlessly focused on business success 24 x 7, but that focus is a good thing. This practice has been highly successful for one wealthy businessman, and his lesson on focus to me was a simple discussion of pointing out that I needed to be more focused…not so "shotgun" slanted.

If we are doing too many things it can be a big distraction. *Combine efforts, utilize others talents, delegate certain tasks, do away with energy zapping thinking and exercises, hone your skills and your focus and come up with a shorter list of things to accomplish.*

Proverbs Chapter 2

Verses 1-3: *My son, if thou wilt receive my words, and hide my commandments with thee; so that thou incline thine ear unto wisdom, and apply thine heart to understanding; yea, if thou criest after knowledge, and liftest up thy voice for understanding.*

These verses have tremendous value to any society. If we listen and keep the words with us, we will be rewarded. If we listen and take action on the instructions given we will be able to apply better direction to our own circumstance.

The final piece to these verses is telling us to seek after knowledge and a better understanding. I believe it has a dual meaning as well: 1) seek wisdom from God, or one who knows all and can affect our lives; and 2) seek other's wisdom. As we gain this knowledge, impart some of it to others, and to our own set of conditions.

Seeking knowledge from God, or *"if thou criest"* after knowledge is a form of praying. This is an ancient tradition carried out by the people of Israel. They would pray as if a child was literally reaching out to a parent for protection, or out of a desire to have something. Many still do pray in this fashion, with arms outstretched to the heavens, and with a loud voice "crying" to God for blessings.

Verse 6: *For the LORD giveth wisdom: out of his mouth cometh knowledge and understanding.*

God wants us to be happy and He wants us to be successful. He will give us wisdom if we sincerely desire it. I believe we must be sincere in our requests to the Lord, and ask Him to bless our performance. If the Creator of the world, and the Creator of us for that matter, is willing to give us wisdom, my only question is "Why wouldn't we listen?"

Since He does not speak to us directly, where are we supposed to find the wisdom that comes from the Lord? Here is a brief list:

1. Scriptures or passages

2. Prayer

3. Inspiration/Feelings

4. Dreams

5. Other writings of Prophets

6. Journal entries/letters from others

7. Parents

8. Wise people

9. Experience (circumstances placed in our way)

10. Children

As you have probably noticed with this short list, most of the wisdom that comes from the Lord, actually comes through others. The first answer on the list is Passages. Prophets have written down what they were inspired to write

> **Key Point**
>
> Isn't it interesting that seven out of ten areas of where we can receive wisdom from the Lord come from others?

to help us and lay down the processes by which the Lord expects us to follow. Prayer, inspiration and dreams are things between you and the Lord. However, isn't it interesting that seven out of ten areas of where we can receive wisdom from the Lord come from others?

Verses 9-10: *Then shalt thou understand righteousness, and judgment, and equity; yea, every good path. When wisdom entereth into thine heart, and knowledge is pleasant unto thy soul; discretion shall preserve thee, understanding shall keep thee.*

Understanding righteousness and judgment is something that few actually acquire in this life. *"Discretion shall preserve"* thee is a phrase that should be carved in stone. But, what does *discretion* actually mean?

The word "discretion" has a few "cousins" that help to describe what that word actually means, with a few similar meanings. Some of these close meanings are: carefulness; judgment; prudence; caution; maturity; diplomacy; tact; responsibility.

We would all do well to exercise a little discretion in our communications with others. Discretion is a sign of maturity as we take on some form of responsibility when we converse with others. The written word and the spoken word are often confused with mixed signals, and we as human beings do not always communicate our true feelings. Excellent advice from a highly successful king.

Verses 11-15: *Discretion shall preserve thee, understanding shall keep thee: to deliver thee from the way of the evil man, from the man that speaketh froward things; who leave the paths of uprightness, to walk in the ways of darkness; who rejoice to do evil, and delight in the frowardness of the wicked; whose ways are crooked, and they froward in their paths.*

Think things through and take inventory of your gut feeling. If it feels right, or good, then do it. If there is hesitation and an uneasy feeling, then don't do it—at least not at that moment.

We all meet many people in our lives that talk a good game, but they may have another agenda entirely different than ours. Their ways are selfish and they only wish to use others to get what they want. I have met, and have been in business with, individuals who fit this mold who will stop at nothing—including blatantly and openly telling falsehoods, to get personal gain.

When a person delights in malice, it doesn't have to be one of the big "transgressions", it can be something as simple as cheating on a test; turning in false numbers; spreading gossip; and not exercising integrity in all that they do.

So the key to understanding this passage is to understand that these types of actions are not on the straight and narrow (or crooked). *A straight path gets you where you want to go faster and with less irritation.*

Verses 20-22: *That thou mayest walk in the way of good men, and keep the paths of the righteous. For the upright shall dwell in the land, and the perfect shall remain in it. But the wicked shall be cut off from the earth, and the transgressors shall be rooted out of it.*

These verses offer a clear indication that those who do what the Lord expects of them (like keeping the commandments) will be blessed. On the flip side, the wicked shall be excluded from those same blessings.

This gets back to our discussion about fearing God. If we fear God and keep His commandments He will, at His discretion, open doors for us and the blessings will flow. This may come after much struggle and turmoil, but the blessings will come. Of this I am especially confident. Life is not easy. It was not meant to be, and it is up to us to turn obstacles into opportunities.

Proverbs Chapter 3

Verses 5-7 *Trust in the LORD with all thine heart; and lean not unto thine own understanding. In all thy ways acknowledge him, and he shall direct thy paths. Be not wise in thine own eyes: fear the LORD, and depart from evil.*

I could write volumes on these verses because I have referred to them many times over the past couple of decades. Solomon's wisdom certainly shines bright in these passages because they give us counsel that has transcended over 3,000 years and still provide an enormous value. These passages are also the motivation that I needed to write this book.

The message is simple and straight forward: *God is wiser that you and me, and He knows what is best for us. In most cases we are independent beings and like to do things on our own.* We even feel like we know our selves better than anyone—including God. The sad reality is that we do not know ourselves better than God, and we could all use a good dose of humbling now and then.

There is also an interesting cross reference to this passage found in Romans Ch. 12 verse 16 it reads: *"Be of the same mind one toward another. Mind not high things, but condescend to men of low estate. Be not wise in your own conceits."* I believe verse seven is instructing us to recognize God's hand in all things.

Verses 9-12: *Honor the LORD with thy substance, and with the firstfruits of all thine increase: so shall thy barns be filled with plenty, and thy presses shall burst out with new wine. My son, despise not the chastening of the LORD; neither be weary of his correction: for whom the LORD loveth he correcteth; even as a father the son in whom he delighteth.*

In ancient times the people of Israel were expected to honor God when they experienced an increase in their wealth. We should always do the same and give thanks to God when we are blessed. When we do give thanks we shall be blessed. Just like any parent who does something nice for their children, we like to be thanked…so does the Lord.

The second part of these passages is a little less easy to be grateful for, simply because we don't like to be corrected when we screw up. When the correcting is done with love and with less anger, it is more bearable. Still we need to be grateful for the opportunity to learn from our mistakes, and to take that learning and put it to good use.

Proverbs Chapter 4

Verses 5-7: *Get wisdom, get understanding: forget it not; neither decline from the words of my mouth. Forsake her not, and she shall preserve thee: love her, and she shall keep thee. Wisdom is the principal thing; therefore get wisdom: and with all thy getting, get understanding.*

The counsel of "getting wisdom" is certainly solid advice. Far too often we have our own agenda's and our list of personal items that we want to follow. The part of this that is interesting, has us believing sometimes that our *schema* is the only thing that matters and we somehow end up forgetting about others. Getting wisdom comes from two things: 1) Learning from others; and 2) making our own prudent decisions.

So then, we must pose the question, "If we exercise wisdom can we actually be preserved?" I believe so. The real question is *"Preserved from what?"* The answer lies in several areas.

- Preserved from financial ruin if you exercise good judgment on basic financial decisions, and not going into debt over your head.

- Preserved from a financial scandal by using wisdom in reporting accurate and real numbers, and staying away from deals that will call into question your integrity and honor.

- Preserved from incarceration if you keep the law.

- Preserved from sadness if you exercise wisdom in being obedient to God's laws.

- Preserved from being homeless by getting an education, or learning a trade and finding a job.

- Preserved from death if you are prudent with your judgment in staying out high danger areas.

- Preserved from an auto accident by staying within the speed limit, and following the rules and signs of the road.

- Preserved from divorce by first marrying the right person, and second by exercising wisdom when differences arise; and communicate in a non-selfish manner.

- Preserved from the embarrassment of walking in late to an important meeting by managing your time better and leaving earlier.

- Preserved from a life of misery if you don't participate in drug use—casual or heavy.

- Preserved from serious HR challenges within the organization if you follow the written policies and procedures.

There is a root Latin word that means to preserve or make safe: *salva or salvus*. The meanings of the word salva are:

Safe

1. Unlikely to cause or result in harm, injury, or damage.

2. In a position or situation that offers protection, so that harm, damage, loss, or unwanted tampering is unlikely.

3. Etymology: from "uninjured, unharmed", from Old French *sauf*, from Latin *salvus*, "uninjured, healthy, safe", related to *salus*, "good health", *saluber*, "healthful".

Safely

With safety; in a safe manner.

Safety

1. Protection from, or not being exposed to, the risk of harm or injury a safety device

2. The inability to cause or to result in harm, injury, or damage.

3. A place or situation where harm, damage, or loss is unlikely.

4. The fact of being or remaining unharmed, uninjured, or undamaged.

Salvage

1. To save used, damaged, or rejected goods for recycling or for further use.

2. To save something of worth or merit from a situation or event that is otherwise a failure

3. To save a ship, cargo, crew, or other property or goods from destruction or loss.

One aspect above that poses an interesting argument is item #2 under "salvage"… *To save something of worth or merit from a situation or event that is otherwise a failure.* I would argue that you and I are "of worth", and if or when we don't exercise wisdom we can end up a failure if we are not careful. Isn't it nice to know that if that were to happen, someone may come along and save us from failure…? It's sort of like a safety net – just in case we fall.

Verses 13-15: *Take fast hold of instruction; let her not go: keep her; for she is thy life. Enter not into the path of the wicked, and go not in the way of evil men. Avoid it, pass not by it, turn from it, and pass away.*

How many times do we have an occasion to learn something

new? If we have not learned something new each day, then the day is wasted. What does it do for us in learning something new each day? It will not only provide new found knowledge, it also keeps the cobwebs out of your brain.

The second part of this discussion is simple: *pass by evil and do not participate in it, and stay away from those who are evil, or in other words, those who could cause you or your family harm due to their actions.* There is plenty of evil in the world, but why do we need to participate in it? Forget about the religious side of the equation for just one moment, and what God you or I may believe in. Focus more on the humanitarian side of things and what it means to be a part of the human race.

We are all humans living on this planet together (even though many people choose to act like animals at times). I realize we can't change everyone to believe that it would be a good thing to live in peace and harmony. But we can make a conscious effort to do what is right and be good to other human beings.

Verse 24: *Put away from thee a froward mouth, and perverse lips put far from thee.*

The counsel here is to basically talk nice and communicate like adults. Far too many times we have a communication break down and the results can be anywhere from minimal to catastrophic.

Sticks and stones may break my bones but words will never hurt me is good advice to follow, but in reality never seems to work in real life amid the hustle and bustle of day-to-day living. I have seen so many feelings hurt that are the result of the spoken and written word. I have seen people get fired for saying mean, and ugly things about others.

The Wisdom of Solomon in this context is a direct hit again. Don't say anything about someone that could come back to haunt you, may be the true message here.

An entire industry called Human Resources exists today to help with the communication process to from employer to employee. Whether at work or at home, poor communication can not only create a bad impression, but can lead to conflict, which can then lead to a negative experience for all parties in the communication process.

Think about a situation where you felt you were on the receiving end of bad communication. How did it make you feel?

Lack of communication or poor communication can lead to:

- Frustration

- Confusion

- Anger

- Mistrust

Better communication can have a positive impact on the organization

For the employee:

- Employee feels more involved/empowered in their job

- Increased understanding and recall

- Happier employee

- More efficient organization

- Higher morale

For the Manager:

- Increased job satisfaction

- Decreased complaints

- Savings in time

- More accurate and efficient employee interviews

What are the causes of poor communication? There are several factors that can cause communication to break down, such as time pressures or a noisy environment. However, a skilled communicator will recognize these factors and try to minimize the negative impact they can have on the communication process.

- Cultural factors

- "Noise"

- Time pressures

- Lack of skills

- Ability/disability

- Environment

There are things that can go wrong at each part of the communication process, which might interfere with the intended meaning of the message.

Message Sent - was the correct language used, was jargon used, was the person sending the message credible, was the medium appropriate, how was the message sent, when was it sent, where was it sent to?

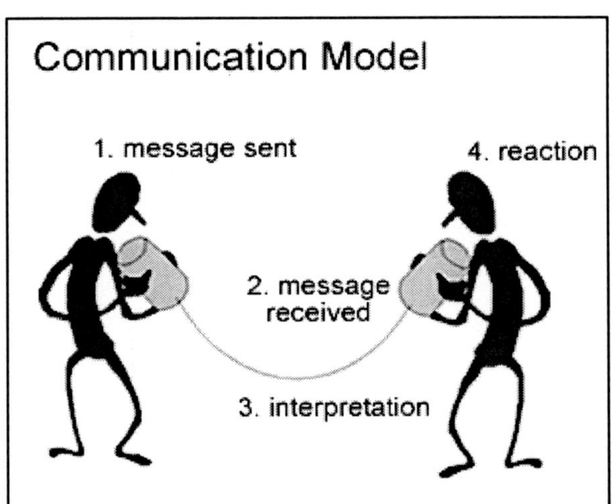

Message Received - did the message get there?

Interpretation - Was the message misinterpreted? Was there a lack of clarity? What personal experiences or cultural values might the recipient have imposed on the message?

Reaction - did you get the reaction you wanted? Was there a smile, blank look, heated argument, and what was the body language?

A few follow-on words of advice: You can increase the likelihood that the message is received and interpreted as you intended by enhancing your communication skills using the following behavior.

- Take care to make messages non-offensive

- Try to communicate the message in a number of different ways - would a visual or an image enhance communications?

- Try to make connections between what the recipient of the message already knows and what are new concepts

- Look for clues as to the persons understanding - both verbal and non-verbal

- Make sure you check for understanding throughout the communication process

- Provide as much clarity as possible

Proverbs Chapter 6

Verses 16-19: *These six things doth the LORD hate; yea, seven are an abomination unto him: a proud look, a lying tongue, and hands that shed innocent blood, a heart that deviseth wicked imaginations, feet that be swift in running to mischief, a false witness that speaketh lies, and he that soweth discord among brethren.*

All of this is good advice no matter what the age or season. But let's focus some attention to the seventh piece of advice *"and he that soweth discord among brethren."*

First, make no mistake all of these are destructive, and all are not what a good person should be engaged in. But think of the first clause and how all other points flow from it. Sowing discord among your brethren is the beginning act that others make a stand from.

Discord is defined as: conflict; friction; argument; and disharmony. The key is to follow the opposite direction than *sowing discord*, and to either stay to yourself, or make a commitment to help others.

Proverbs Chapter 8

Verse 11: *For wisdom is better than rubies; and all the things that may be desired are not to be compared to it.*

If you had all the rubies in the world, you would certainly be very wealthy. But is that all that you would have? Money can't buy happiness as they say, but it does buy many things in this life. The real question lies within the term of what it actually cannot buy for you.

Think of the things money cannot buy, because the list is long. And, think of the many things in this life that everyone can take advantage of whether rich or poor. At the top of the list I have listed Happiness, because there are plenty of miserable millionaires in the world today. Consider these important things that money cannot buy:

- Happiness

- Wisdom

- Knowledge

- Good health

- A sound mind

- Good weather

- True love

- Loyal friends

- Clean water

- Fresh air

- A child's smile

- The warmth of holding hands

- The friendship of a good dog

- A clear night with a billion stars

- A full moon

- A spring rain

- December snow

- Sweat smells of an April morning

- The beauty of a flower

- The song of a bird

- A hike in the mountains

- A talk with your grandpa

- Quiet, sacred moments in church

- The feeling of helping someone in need

- Jumping into a pile of autumn leaves

- The sounds of the ocean

- A walk in the summer rain

- A high school band practicing in the distance

- The sound of a jet passing overhead

- The laughter of children

- The smell of fresh cut cedar

- A quiet walk with the one you love

- The beauty of a fall rose

- The serene beauty of miles of tulips in a field

- The sounds of a bubbling brook

- The wind rustling the leaves of trees

- The joy of holding your first child

- The flight of an eagle

- A burning flame

- The flicker of a candle

Verse 33: *Hear instruction, and be wise, and refuse it not.*

How many times have each of us received counsel and have refused it because we thought we knew a better way, or had it all figured out? I believe I am pretty safe in saying that I am not the only one on planet earth that has received wise counsel and has refused to listen. My parents gave me very wise counsel growing up, many, many times, and for the most part I listened. But because I am a little "strong willed" and like to be independent at times, I have chosen a different path a time or two, and have learned to regret it.

The older I got, the wiser my parents seemed to get. Isn't that an interesting twist on the psyche of a young man who seemed to have everything all figured out including a plan of action? Sometimes it was the general gut feeling of my parents or other wise individuals in my life that would simply tell me not to pursue that business relationship; or not to go into that particular venture; or to steer clear of a particular individual.

This is an important element that we must consider for a moment. I certainly don't have all of this figured out, but I do know that we need to listen to the counsel of those that are wiser than us, and exercise wisdom more often than we probably do.

Proverbs Chapter 9

Verse 6: *Forsake the foolish and live; and go in the way of understanding.*

This goes hand in hand with the previous verse of learning from those that are wise and have been around the block a few times. Forsaking foolish people, or steering clear of their foolish ways is great counsel. But how do you know if they are foolish, and you shouldn't follow along?

The first thing to realize is the gut feeling that you have: if it is negative, no matter how flamboyant, or rich, or famous, or popular they are—steer clear of corrupt friends. If they don't treat others like you like to be treated, then what makes you think they will treat you any different? Sooner or later their true colors will come out, and hopefully you will not be standing next to them or in their path, because they will forget you, and only think of themselves.

> **Key Point**
>
> The first thing to realize is the gut feeling that you have: if it is negative, no matter how flamboyant, or rich, or famous, or popular they are—steer clear of corrupt friends.

Verses 10-12: *The fear of the LORD is the beginning of wisdom: and the knowledge of the Holy is understanding. For by me thy days shall be multiplied, and the years of thy life shall be increased. If thou be wise, thou shalt be wise for thyself: but if thou scornest, thou alone shalt bear it.*

What great counsel, and what tremendous blessings await those who worship God and follow His counsel! Who would have thought that exercising wisdom would actually increase the number of days or years of life?

Could it be as simple as wise people don't take ill-advised risks that could put them in danger…physical, financial, emotional? Perhaps. Or could it also be as simple as a loving God wanting His children to be successful, and the key to success is obedience? These obviously are rhetorical questions and I don't expect an answer from you, but spend a few moments thinking this concept out.

Think about those who dabble in the recreational use of drugs. It may start out as something for fun, but very soon the addiction takes hold and the person is left to fight a terrible monster, one that will be extremely difficult to overcome. This may even be life threatening in many cases, and downright perilous in most cases.

And what about a person who decides to gamble a little here and there, winning once in a while, just enough to keep them coming back. Then before they know it they are addicted to gambling and may end up borrowing money to cover their debts, and the downward spiral in their finances begins.

Of course there are hundreds of examples that could be cited here, but you can see how these types of unwise decisions can lead to personal and business peril. It could even be as simple as the stress that unwise decisions cause and the hours or years that stress may take off one's life.

So, scorning wise counsel can be detrimental at best, if not positively fatal in some cases.

Proverbs Chapter 10

Verse 1: *A wise son maketh a glad father: but a foolish son is the heaviness of his mother.*

I am a son to wonderful parents. My Mom and Dad are the salt of the earth and amazing examples of everything a parent or grandparent should aspire to become. I always wanted to please my father and my mother in every way, and have always felt it important to do my best to make them proud of me. Whenever I have made stupid choices and have brought shame or reason to doubt on our family name it has made me queasy.

Today I have six children of my own, and it is such a joy to see them do well and make good choices. I cringe and even cry to see them make dumb decisions that cause themselves, or others harm. This particular verse is very true…wise children make happy parents.

Solomon was the son of David and made his father proud of the things he did growing up. He was his favorite son, and followed in his father's footsteps in being wise in building up his kingdom. But like his father, Solomon also made poor decisions. Solomon's biggest downfall was that he married outside of his people, and took on many wives from foreign countries.

David's downfall was twofold: his own lust for Bathsheba, then his very unwise decision to cover up his affair with Bathsheba by sending her husband Uriah to front lines of the battle. Uriah would not return home to be with his wife as David had commanded, because he could not bear to leave his men fighting the battle with the Philistines…while he would have comfort at home with his wife. Thus, David sent him to the front lines of the battle knowing he stood a very high chance of being killed.

But for a time, both of these kings were very wise in building their empires…especially Solomon.

How many times have we read about sons (and daughters) that have caused grief to their parents for one reason or another? The thousands of *poor* examples that I could cite would get boring all too soon. The primary reason any of those examples would become boring is that they are centered on two words: **selfish pride**. Once this infection creeps into anyone's life it is difficult to see that is a cancer that spreads and takes over deductive decision making, but even harder to get rid of.

> **Definition**
>
> Selfish pride can be defined as "excessive confidence or glorification in one's self, possessions or nation." The concept is found in the Bible, along with pride itself, in words such as arrogance, haughtiness and conceit, among others, all of which are opposite of Godly humility.

Selfish pride can be defined as "excessive confidence or glorification in one's self, possessions or nation." The concept is found in the Bible, along with pride itself, in words such as arrogance, haughtiness and conceit, among others, all of which are opposite of Godly humility. The wrongness of self-centered pride is essentially twofold. On a spiritual level, it inevitably leads to disregard, disrespect and disobedience to God.

On a worldly level, selfish pride very often results in self-destructive behavior because, while a form of self-delusion, it isn't necessarily as much an *over*estimation of one's self as it is a dangerous *under*estimation of others, hence "Pride goes before destruction, and a haughty spirit before a fall" (Proverbs 16:18). The Bible also speaks of a *good* pride, but it differs greatly from selfish pride.

Verse17: *He is in the way of life that keepeth instruction: but he that refuseth reproof erreth.*

This is a fun, but old way of saying "listen to counsel and learn from constructive critique". I will be the first to admit that I hate it when I have been "reproved", or told that I need to improve on something.

In life we sometimes do not make the best choices and we somehow get caught in situations that require sound judgment. When we don't make the best choice and we are held responsible for our actions it is then up to us to figure out what we will do going forward. And, when someone comes down on us for our incorrect choices, it becomes our problem that we must own up to—not only own up to, but vow to never make the same poor choice again.

During the nineties I was operating a successful manufacturing business that required a lot of attention to manufacturing details, as well as other details that any other small business requires. Things like: employees, customers, brand building, on-time delivery, supply chain management and a myriad of other things that come with running a small business, needed to be a clear focal point of everyone in the company.

There was a certain young man that was just going through the motions and not paying attention to details in assembling one of our products. Our products were vending machines, and each one had a certain pattern that needed to be followed while assembling the area where the coins dropped. This needed to be a highly secure area since theft could be made almost impossible if the system was followed during the assembly phase. If the process wasn't followed properly, criminals could eventually figure out where the weaknesses were and get to the coins much easier.

It wasn't until a few months had passed, and we started receiving reports of the machines being vandalized in L.A. County in California. Several thefts of our machines had occurred all within a fifty mile radius, and all at the same point of entry. This seemed odd, so I went back to the ship dates, and they were all shipped within one week. Then, I went to the assembly log and the same individual had worked on all of the machines. When questioned, the employee said he was having a bad week at the time the machines were made, and that he had been told by the supervisor that his workmanship was not up to par. The supervisor also added that the employee didn't like the way he was scolded, but that he had vowed to never do it again. We made the replacement parts and shipped them out to the owner of the 25 machines.

All seemed to be settled satisfactory to all parties involved. The employee was reproved, and although he did not like the scolding, he enjoyed his job and the work environment, and really wanted to continue working for us. The customer was happy that we acted so quickly to repair the problem, and we sent him extra candy products at no charge.

Hindsight is always 20/20 and I should have fired him after the first instance. This later happened again, and the next incident was more severe. My company was facing a lawsuit from an angry customer (an attorney) who claimed that we had purposely manufactured an inferior product, and that he was out thousands of dollars due to shoddy workmanship. That part was easy to solve because we would never intend to purposely manufacture an inferior product. We sent replacement parts and extra product at no charge again, and the customer was eventually happy, and the lawsuit was dropped.

Only now I had to deal with the employee that made the same mistake again. I ended up firing him, and it was not an easy thing to do since he was the nephew of one of our other employees. He begged and pleaded not to let him go, but he left me no choice: his actions had proved otherwise harmful to the company, and he made the choice himself by refusing the counsel given earlier. It was the same mistake that he had made before, and he felt like he knew more than his supervisor, and therein laid his error. Plus, we have to go back to principle #7 pointed out in Chapter 2: "Hold Others Accountable."

Proverbs Chapter 11

Verse 9: *A hypocrite with his mouth destroyeth his neighbor: but through knowledge shall the just be delivered.*

Without getting too political here, how many times do we read in the news that people in politics will do just about anything to either get elected, or to stay in office--especially during an election year? All too often political candidates will stretch the truth; their campaign managers will dig up dirt on other candidates just to create a diversion; or their advisors may even go to such great lengths as stealing classified documents then lie about it. This happens on both sides of the fence, be it Republican, Democrat, or Independent...so no one party is not necessarily holding a pitchfork, while the other wears a halo.

Take the hypocrisy case in point of Sandy Berger, who was the National Security Advisor to President Bill Clinton. Mr. Berger stole highly classified terrorism documents from the National Archives, destroyed them and lied to investigators, and is still an adviser to presidential candidates. Berger, who was fired from John Kerry's presidential campaign when the scandal broke in 2004, had assumed a similar role in Hillary Clinton's campaign. His security clearance was suspended until September 2008.

The Justice Department initially said Berger stole only copies of classified documents and not originals. But the House Government Reform Committee later revealed that an unsupervised Berger had been given access to classified files of original, un-copied, un-inventoried documents on terrorism. Several Archives officials acknowledged that Berger could have stolen any number of items and they "would never know what, if any, original documents were missing."

At his sentencing in September 2005, Berger was fined $50,000, placed on probation for two years and stripped of his security clearance for three years. Anyone else would have been given 15 years in prison. Sometimes those in politics seem to have a fuzzy memory of events that could cause them or their country harm.

Berger stuffed highly classified documents into his pants and socks before hauling them out of the Archives building in Washington, according to investigators. On one occasion, upon reaching the street, he hid documents under a construction trailer after checking the windows of the Archives and Justice Department buildings to make sure he was not being watched.

He came back later and retrieved the documents, taking them home and cutting them up with scissors—sounds like a well-written spy thriller!

Berger also lied to the public, telling reporters he made an "honest mistake" by "inadvertently" taking the documents, which he blamed on his own "sloppiness." President Bill Clinton vouched for the explanation for Berger, who served as his national security adviser.

"Politicians are sometimes so steeped in hypocrisy it makes it difficult to keep a straight face when leaders talk about a "culture of corruption." (Source: Oct 8, 2007 by Bill Sammon, The Examiner).

What of the hypocrisy that we see in the news about celebrities who seem to be above the law as well? There are just some things that we cannot change, but we can focus on ourselves, and even our family to stay away from destructive hypocrisy.

Verse 12: *He that is void of wisdom despiseth his neighbor: but a man of understanding holdeth his peace.*

I believe Solomon was trying to tell us that wise neighbors help each other, rather than hurt each other. Even when our neighbors offend us, the wiser person will have a talk with them and discuss the problem. According to Solomon when we don't take measures to work with our neighbors, and sometimes even hold our tongue, we are completely void of wisdom.

Verse16: *...and strong men retain riches.*

The area of being strong for men is certainly intriguing. According to Solomon, if you are strong you are eligible to retain riches. I believe it is for those who are **valiant** in their defense of many good things: family, country, religion, friends. Being strong for those things in life are certainly noble causes, and I believe will be blessed for their efforts.

Verse 17: *The merciful man doeth good to his own soul: but he that is cruel troubleth his own flesh.*

Once again getting back to the idea of *treating others like you would like to be treated* is sound advice and probably doesn't require much more discussion. But indulge me for just a moment.

Not to simplify this concept too much, but being merciful: GOOD; being cruel: NOT GOOD. I certainly don't mean to insult your intelligence, but there are a lot of people in the world due to selfish reasons, may turn to the cruel side to get what they want.

I probably don't need to point out the obvious, but I will: If we would show a little more mercy once in a while, then we might be afforded the same type of compassion at a time when we truly need it. And if we are cruel to people then how can we ask for mercy ourselves?

If I yell and scream at my kids all the time, then why should I expect them to always be quiet, nice, little angels, or to treat their friends with respect? If I spend like a crazy fool and do not save anything along the way, then why should I expect to have a large savings account? The same is true for how we treat others…being merciful: Good; being cruel: Not good.

Proverbs Chapter 12

Verse 1: *Whoso loveth instruction loveth knowledge: but he that hateth reproof is brutish.*

I love to learn. It is like a never ending fountain that we can go to and be satisfied. The instruction I receive from my parents; my wife and children; good teachers; God-fearing men and women; and yes, even scholars, is like being a fed a full course meal at Thanksgiving when you have not eaten for a full day.

But, I must admit again, I have a lot to learn about receiving constructive criticism, or being reproved. My pride seems to get in the way, and it takes a little extra convincing that the admonition to do something different is constructive, and not just scolding.

Where are you with this concept? Do you encourage others to give you guidance or counsel on improving your situation…your life? I guess it also comes down to the method used in the reproof. Maybe it just simply comes down to the increase showing of, dare I say love and concern? If someone reprimands me and gives guidance and counsel at the same time, I am more apt to listen to what they have to say without taking offense.

The key here is to try and peel through to the true meaning of the reproof, and figure how best to use the counsel.

Verse 11: *He that tilleth his land shall be satisfied with bread: but he that followeth vain persons is void of understanding.*

Now this cuts right to the chase on the topic of working for a living. I like what Solomon offers here, and agree wholeheartedly with the concept of putting in an honest days work for an honest days pay.

Teenagers and oft times, "kids" into their early 30's today have a warped view of acquiring assets: they want it all now…things that have taken their parents 20-40 years to achieve, they want right now. It doesn't help when you have companies throwing around credit like it was manna from heaven.

I see far too many young couples that start off their marriage carrying huge debt with a $600,000 house; two brand new vehicles that total $90,000; a household of fine furniture; two memberships to the most exclusive spa in town; eating out every night; etc. etc. Where do they get their money from? The fact is in most cases they are living pay check to pay check and 30 days away from losing everything. The fact is they have mortgaged theirs and their children's future. The fact is our society is in deep trouble if we don't do a better job of educating everyone about not working for a living and not putting something aside for a rainy day.

There are also far too many get rich quick schemes to name them all. You know what they are, but have you managed to stay away from them? I can tell you that I have not stayed away from all of them in my lifetime. I've thought, well yeah, I know a lot of people and if I just sign up a few of them this business will build itself! I'm embarrassed to admit that I have fallen prey to a few get rich quick schemes in my life, but I have learned from each experience, and the biggest lesson I have learned is that it is a business, just like any other, and you have to spend time planning, and building and sacrificing to make it work.

If a farmer does not plan ahead prior to the growing season; if he does not prepare the ground and plant the seeds; if he does not water and fertilize the soil; if he does not harvest at the right time; the crops will fail, and he will have no food to sell or to feed his family. If he does not properly till his land, he will fail. This lesson was simple 3,000 years ago, and remains a simple lesson today. We could all learn a thing or two about working by spending 30 minutes with a farmer.

Verse 22: *Lying lips are an abomination to the LORD: but they that deal truly are his delight.*

This too, is wise counsel to follow. Lying causes a myriad of problems that could be avoided by telling the truth. Take a look at why you are lying and you'll find ways to help yourself stop. Don't over promise. Many lies feel necessary because you've gotten yourself into a situation and you don't know how to get out of it. You can start by not over committing yourself with other people. Only promise what you can realistically deliver.

> ### Key Point
>
> If a farmer does not plan ahead prior to the growing season; if he does not prepare the ground and plant the seeds; if he does not water and fertilize the soil; if he does not harvest at the right time; the crops will fail. We could all learn a thing or two about working by spending 30 minutes with a farmer.

The problem of working out who is lying and who is telling the truth is as old as civilization itself. But the idea that a person's truthfulness can be detected, regardless of what they are actually saying, may be not much more than a throwback to ancient ideas of trial by ordeal.

In English medieval courts truth was tested by ordeals of fire and water, on the basis a truthful person would be protected by God. Someone suspected of lying would have to carry a red-hot iron bar for nine paces. Alternatively he could opt to walk across nine red-hot ploughshares. Either way, if the suspect was burned then this was proof that he was lying and so could be promptly hung.

Other courts went in for trial by water. In the ultimate "no-win" situation, the person accused of lying was put into a sack and thrown into a pond. If the accused sank this showed he was innocent, but he might well drown anyway. If he floated this was taken proof that he was lying and he would be hanged. Such practices were ended in 1215 by edict of the Latern Council.

By the 1600s the idea arose that the truth of any statement could be arrived at by the means of detailed questioning and the application of scientific and logical reasoning to what was being said. Modern legal conventions of cross-examination and the presumption that some-body is telling the truth unless it can be proved otherwise "beyond reasonable doubt" date from this time.

Trying to work out whether somebody was lying was a matter of questioning, debate and the clash between different points of view based on the gathering and analysis of evidence. The 19th Century saw a reversion to ideas of truthfulness and lying as moral conditions embedded in the unique personality of the accused person. The new "sciences" of phrenology - measurement of "bumps" on a person's skull - and psychology - led to the idea that lies could be detected by looking at physical symptoms.

The search for "scientific" ways of spotting liars moved from bumps on the head to brain chemistry, with the search for a "truth serum" drug. Barbiturates including scopolamine, sodium amytal and sodium pentothal were given to suspects in the hope that drugs could somehow rewire the brain, making it incapable of telling a deliberate lie.

The "medicine" had the intended effect of causing the victim to lose control over what he was saying. But the result was normally an endless stream of drug-addled gibberish rather than "the truth". In 1963 the US Supreme Court said "serum-induced confession" was in effect a form of torture and the practice was ruled unconstitutional. The latest attempt at scientific detection of truth and falsehood comes, fashionably enough, in the application of sophisticated electronics to the problem.

Makers of the latest lie detector machine - which measures supposedly tell-tale changes in temperature around the eye sockets when somebody is telling a deliberate untruth - claim a "success rate" of 83% in detecting liars.

But whether it will prove any more reliable that conventional "polygraph" lie detectors, which rely on sensors to detect breathing rate, pulse, blood pressure and perspiration, remains open to question.

This is also a continuation of one of the 10 Commandments "Thou shalt not bear false witness against thy neighbor." The best advice is to abstain from lying and you will be much better off.

Proverbs Chapter 13

Verse 1: *A wise son heareth his father's instruction: but a scorner heareth not rebuke.*

I can look back on my experience growing up and the counsel that my father would give me, and think of times when I should have listened more carefully. There are too many to mention, unfortunately, but one in particular was when I was about ten years old. It was a Sunday morning and I was dressed to go to church with my family. My Dad had told me to stay in the back yard and not go over to my buddy's house to play basketball. My buddy Wayne and his brother Jay, were having a great time playing together, and they beckoned me to hop the fence and come over and play. That was all I needed…and over the fence I went.

Ten minutes later my fun ended with Dad standing at the fence yelling for me to get home. That day was not a particularly good day for my Dad for some reason, as he greeted me at the fence with a stern look on his face, and a tone that let me know that he was not happy: "I thought I told you to stay in the yard, and you flat out disobeyed me." This was a cinderblock fence that was six feet high, so I climbed back over into our yard, and when I got to the ground I received a swift swat to the back of my head.

The counsel of a father should always be adhered to no matter how unpopular or passé it may look or sound. My own children sometimes press the envelope to see how far they can take something, and they are not always little angels, but they do respect our counsel.

> ### Key Point
>
> The counsel of a father should always be adhered to no matter how unpopular or passé it may look or sound.

The primary thing is not get to the point of being rebuked.

Verse 10: *Only by pride cometh contention: but with the well advised is wisdom.*

Once again the pride of human beings has a discouraging way of hindering progress. In this case, Solomon advises us that because of pride people contend with one another. The first question is to ask ourselves "Why do we contend with others?" Why do others feel so compelled to contend with you or me? The answer lies in with one additional word that we can add in front of pride, and it is *selfish* pride.

The root of being selfish comes from putting ones own beliefs, values, or ideas first before others. We have discussed this concept in more detail previously, but Solomon felt compelled to remind us again and again throughout the book of Proverbs. Pride is the great destroyer of progress. Pride is the stumbling block of one walking on the straight and narrow. Pride is the great barrier that bars counsel and wise instruction. Why…? Because when we are too full of pride, nothing else matters accept what WE want.

Pride can be summed in five words:

Pleasure – our pleasure over others

Rudeness – being rude to others

Impoliteness – being polite to others simply does not matter

Disrespect – showing disrespect to others

Egotism – our own ego gets in the way

Verse 22: *A good man leaveth an inheritance to his children's children and the wealth of the sinner is laid up for the just.*

One definition of inheritance is: the practice of passing on property, titles, debts, and obligations upon the death of an individual. It has long played an extremely important role in human societies.

Focus on the first section of this verse and leaving an inheritance to children, your children and other children of the world. I believe leaving an inheritance comes down to two elements:

- Financial

- Well-being or Welfare of others

For the financial side of the equation, we need to take a close look at what are we working for, and what have we saved--or created to make life a little better, a little easier for a child. Since our children are our future leaders, inventors, athletes, teachers, scientists, etc., doesn't it make sense to figure out what we are doing now to somehow make a difference in their lives?

If you have children, make sure you leave them something in the way of finances. Get a good life insurance policy and keep it in force. Put a little away each paycheck and build up a savings. Pay off your debts. These are all simple, basic premises to live by, but somehow we as a society have mortgaged our children's future. As of this writing, every man woman and child in America owes over $126,000 to pay down the national debt. That does not include any personal debt that we all have. This is only the debt that America owes other countries, that gets passed on to you, me, our children, and so on. This is pathetic, and we just let it go on, and on.

So what are you doing to secure your children's future and help them with some kind of financial inheritance? I hope you have done, or will do something about this right away.

The second element of an inheritance, or Welfare, is leaving your children with a good memory about you. The fun times you spend together…the teaching moments that you took advantage of…the fun traditions you have established…the holidays and vacation time you spent together. All of these factors in a family life make up lasting memories that shape who we are.

We have an obligation to leave our children a better world, even if that "world" consists of our own home life. There are many things in this life that we can't change right away, but we can have a direct effect on our family life, and we can make a difference with our own children.

I strongly believe that we all can make a difference in a big way as we work together as a society. I also believe that we can be a profound difference in the lives of our very own children. My wife and I have six lives that can be affected by our actions and personal discussions. My kids hopefully have learned a few things from their parents along the way. And, the lives of others are also hopefully affected to the positive as we interact with others outside of our family.

Proverbs Chapter 14

Verse 5: *A faithful witness will not lie; but a false witness will utter lies.*

How may times have you been in situation when someone told a lie about you? Or, have you ever wanted something so bad that you did not tell the truth about someone, or some event, just to make you look good? These are not pleasant experiences, and sometimes the damage can be done for years to come in situations like these.

Solomon's advice is to tell the truth, and live up to one of the 10 Commandments by NOT bearing a false witness against your neighbor. Simple and effective, just the way it ought to be. How are you doing with following this wise counsel? If the answer is to the negative, stop; change course and make amends. You will be much happier in life if you will put away your pride, and stop focusing on what you want all the time.

Verse 21: *He that despiseth his neighbor sinneth; but he that hath mercy on the poor happy is he.*

This verse goes along with verse 5, and not too much more needs to be added. Although it is wise counsel to help the poor and the needy to have a better life. There are billions people in the world that need our help in more ways than one. Instead of focusing on billions, just focus on a few right in your own family; in your home town; in your community. These alone will bring you a lifetime of happiness and satisfaction, and when we all pitch in, can eventually make a difference in the millions.

Verse 29: *He that is slow to wrath is of great understanding; but he that is hasty of spirit exalteth folly.*

Anger management is a great thing to master, and I am the first one that needs to do a better job at this—especially on the highways during traffic. I am working on my patience, but traffic in major cities can be maddening at best. Since I travel to new cities multiple times each month, I have the pleasure of dealing with all kinds of delays, traffic jams, rude drivers, and angry commuters.

My favorite one is when people speed up to get in front of you just to save 2.4 seconds. Several years ago I used to wonder why people in major cities always seem to be on edge, and angry all the time. I thought it was just due to too much crime and pollution…although I'm sure that has something to do with it. I believe traffic is the piece that throws them, all of us, over the edge.

I give you my word to do better, and to work on my impatience and "wrath" when I am driving.

Proverbs Chapter 15

Verse 1: *A soft answer turneth away wrath: but grievous words stir up anger.*

As a carry over to the last verse, this is one of my favorite Proverbs. My wife Ann has this hanging on the wall of our home. We received this Proverb embroidered on a lace picture that is framed and hanging in our living room.

> ### Key Point
>
> We would all do better to take the higher road and to hold our anger for a brief moment and think through our answer without giving off an aura of being angry.

I don't remember who gave us this wall piece, but it was, and still is wise counsel for newlyweds to work things out without raising our voices. Come to think of it this is wise counsel for newlyweds all the way through to nearly-deads. We would all do better to take the higher road and to hold our anger for a brief moment and think through our answer without giving off an aura of being angry.

Many times with my children I have wanted to raise my voice to get my point across. And, unfortunately I have raised my voice. Not that this is always a bad thing... I don't believe we can always be completely passive when a child is out of control, but I have needed to do a better job on holding my anger. I am happy to say that I have never struck my children, although I have had to leave the house and count to 100 on a few occasions!

As we have sat down and discussed a problem together, even pointed out the faults of one another, we have always left saying "I love you", and a renewed confidence that it was a learning moment and we learned new things of what not to do and how to better handle the situation.

It has been when I let my pride get in the way and did raise my voice, that the child would become scared or defensive, and even angry.

Sometimes I feel that even when my daughters are having a bad day and they are snapping at everyone, that the mood of the house is different. We want to be treated with respect and a snappy, curt answer does indeed set us off, and make us angry.

Countries would get along better; families would be more loving; *the workplace would be much more productive if we would just learn to follow Solomon's counsel: to tone it down a notch or two, and give a soft answer.*

Proverbs Chapter 16

Verse 7: *When a man's ways please the Lord, he maketh even his enemies to be at peace with him.*

Let's face it bad things happen to good people and sometimes we simply can't avoid adversity in our lives. But if our actions are those that are aligned with the commandments and expectations of the Lord, we will eventually have His favor on our side.

This is where faith and hope come into play that a brighter day is ahead of us if our hearts, and our actions are right with God. Is it possible to call upon a Supreme Being and ask for help out of a jam, whether personal, or in business? The simple answer is a resounding "yes", but let's go a little deeper.

Our responsibility is to do everything in our power to make things right; to communicate; to work like the dickens to make something come to pass, and when we have done everything we can—living the laws of the land—we have the right to ask for blessings. We have the right to also ask for a miracle.

Do miracles in business exist today? You bet they do. In small business, simple survival might be considered a miracle. Small business owners and entrepreneurs are miracle workers and they come up with the coolest products and services to make life better for us all. There are inventions in the past 25 years that are truly miraculous that have been invented and perfected by small businesses. To name a few:

- The personal computer
- Laptops
- 24 inch monitors
- Jump sticks that hold 8 gig of data on a two inch stick
- Cell phones
- The Internet
- Email
- Online shopping
- Voice mail
- The Fax machine
- Blackberry's
- iPhones
- Software that makes all this stuff work
- Bandwidth to transport data
- Computer Networking
- Printers
- Copiers
- CD's
- DVD's
- Robotics in manufacturing

- Laser machines that cut metal

- Lasik surgery

- Light bulbs that last 10 years

- Computerized dishwashers

- Refrigerators with ice and water in the door

- Microwave ovens

- Cable television

- Satellite television

- Satellite radio

- Portable heaters

Think about the advances in technology and medicine during the last 100; 50; 25; 5 years. I touched on this earlier in the book, but just how technology seems to reinvent itself every 5 years now. We wouldn't dream of owning a 5 year old computer or cell phone. It is old technology and the software designed for these devices today does not work on older units. These modern inventions are truly miraculous, and I know they were inspired by a higher source.

What about medicine? Take a look at the top things that have been accomplished in medicine during the 20th century:

- Placebo-controlled, randomized, blinded clinical trials became a powerful tool for testing new medicines.

- Antibiotics drastically reduced mortality from bacterial diseases and their prevalence.

- A vaccine was developed for polio, ending a worldwide epidemic. Effective vaccines were also developed for a number of other serious infectious diseases, including diphtheria, pertussis (whooping cough), tetanus, measles, mumps, rubella

(German measles), chickenpox, influenza, hepatitis A, and hepatitis B.

- A successful application of epidemiology and vaccination led to the eradication of the smallpox virus in humans.

- X-rays became a powerful diagnostic tool for wide spectrum of diseases, from bone fractures to cancer. In the 1960s, computerized tomography was invented. Other important diagnostics tools developed were sonography and magnetic resonance imaging.

- Development of vitamins virtually eliminated scurvy and other vitamin-deficiency diseases.

- New psychiatric drugs were developed. This includes anti-psychotics which are efficient in treating hallucinations and delusions, and antidepressants for treating depression.

- The role of tobacco smoking the #1 cause of lung cancer and other diseases was proven during the 1950s.

- New methods for cancer treatment, including chemotherapy, radiation therapy, and immunotherapy, were developed. As a result, cancer could often be cured or placed in remission.

- The development of blood typing and blood banking made blood transfusion safe and widely available.

- The invention and development of immunosuppressive drugs and tissue typing made organ and tissue transplantation a clinical reality.

- As research on all aspects of sleep and circadian rhythms exploded, dozens of sleep disorders were defined.

- New methods for heart surgery were developed. Cardiac surgery is surgery on the heart and/or great vessels performed by a cardiac surgeon. Frequently, it is done to treat complications of heart disease (for example, coronary artery bypass grafting), correct congenital heart disease, or treat heart disease created by various causes including endocarditis. It also includes heart transplantation.

- Cocaine and heroin were found to be dangerous addictive drugs, and their wide usage has been outlawed.

- Contraceptive drugs were developed, which reduced population growth rates.

- The development of medical insulin during the 1920s helped raise the life expectancy of diabetics to three times of what it had been earlier.

- The elucidation of the structure and function of DNA initiated the development of genetic engineering and the mapping of the human genome.

- Source: Wikipedia Encyclopedia, December 2007

So, getting back to the original verse, when we do what God expects of us, we are entitled to ask for and receive blessings. One of those blessings could even be that our enemy's heart can be softened. Wouldn't it be great if political leaders could catch this vision and encourage the people of their countries to pray to God and ask for help?

Verse 18: *Pride goeth before destruction, and an haughty spirit before the fall.*

Putting ourselves before God in any capacity will eventually spell disaster for us, whether in business, or in our personal lives. Pride is the great stumbling block in our society as it was in Solomon's time.

With pride our focus is only upon ourselves…not on God or on others for that matter. **Pride** is the name of an emotion which refers to joy in the accomplishments of oneself; thinking of self higher than anyone and everyone else. According to the Concise Oxford Dictionary, *Proud* comes from late Old English *prud*, probably from Old French *prude* "brave, valiant" (11th century), from Latin *prode* "advantageous, profitable", from *prodesse* "be useful". The sense of "having a high opinion of oneself", not in French, may reflect the Anglo-Saxons' opinion of the Norman knights who called themselves "proud", like the French knights *preux*.

Definition

Pride is the name of an emotion which refers to joy in the accomplishments of oneself; thinking of self higher than anyone and everyone else. The sense of "having a high opinion of oneself." It is considered one of the seven deadly sins.

In religion, Pride (also Vanity or *arrogance*) is the essentially competitive and excessive belief in one's own abilities that interferes with the individual's recognition of the grace of God, or the worth which God sees in others; for example: *"In his Pride the wicked does not seek Him; in all his thoughts there is no room for God."* (Psalm 10:4) Pride is also one of the 7 deadly sins: (Pride, Envy, Lust, Wrath, Sloth, Gluttony and Greed).

The best advice here is to recognize the source of our successes, and to give praise to the Almighty in our personal lives and in business.

Proverbs Chapter 17

Verse 6: *Children's children are the crown of old men; and the glory of children are their fathers.*

I have to say something here about my own children, and how they truly are the crowning milestone of their parents. I love my six children and would do anything for them, including lay down my life. We love to see them succeed in life, and win at life's battles. They are bombarded with so many things on a daily basis that I did not have to deal with as I was growing up. I'm not so sure that I would be strong enough to not succumb to some of the degenerate things they face on a regular basis. I love and respect them for their choices and their good-natured ways about them.

So how do our children make it in life, and how do we prepare them to be our future leaders? I look at how my children choose to follow our example in many things: our religion; our political choices; the way we treat others; how we communicate with one another; the lifestyle we are accustomed to; the path we follow in life; etc. Thank goodness for a virtuous woman, their mother, that teaches them so many good things.

The first thing to think about long and hard is what type of example we are setting for our children. If we are doing things that inspire others, then hopefully that will rub off on to our kids, and they will be inspiring to their own generation. If we are not acting in a way that is pleasing to our Supreme Being, then we need to re-evaluate what we are doing.

What if what we are doing actually does have eternal consequences? I believe they do have eternal, not just for this life, but eternal—life after this life, consequences. And, I also want my parents to be proud of me for my accomplishments; and for the way I treat others. I would curl up in the fetal position and melt into a pile of mush if I were to hear my father say that he was disappointed in me and my actions. That would be utterly devastating to me. So in essence I live my life because I feel that I will answer to my earthly father, and to my Heavenly Father.

Does that translate over to business practices? It should…and it should be on our minds each and every day as we transact business.

Verse 28: *Even a fool, when he holdeth his peace, is counted wise: and he that shutteth his lips is esteemed a man of understanding.*

How wise is it to hold our tongue and to listen? I have talked about this several times already, but holding our tongue once in a while is not only a sign of great maturity, it also is a sign that we have swallowed our own selfish pride somewhere along the way.

That is the great challenge…and I challenge you to exercise strength and shut your lips as Solomon has counseled, when things get a little heated. You will be the benefactor of a promise made by a highly successful king, and be esteemed as a person of understanding.

Proverbs Chapter 19

Verse 15: *Slothfulness casteth into a deep sleep; and an idle soul shall suffer hunger.*

Also considered to be one of the 7 Deadly Sins, being slothful is simply not a good island to inhabit.

From the **Pocket Catholic Catechism**:

> *Sloth is the desire for ease, even at the expense of doing the known will of God. Whatever we do in life requires effort. Everything we do is to be a means of salvation. The slothful person is unwilling to do what God wants because of the effort it takes to do it. Sloth becomes a sin when it slows down and even brings to a halt the energy we must expend in using the means to salvation*
>
> Medieval theologian Thomas Aquinas said Sloth is "sluggishness of the mind which neglects to begin good... [it] is evil in its effect, if it so oppresses man as to draw him away entirely from good deeds." (2,35, ad 1)

Source: Pocket Catholic Catechism

<table><tr><td>

Definition

The slothful person is unwilling to do what God wants because of the effort it takes to do it.

</td><td>

The opposite of sloth is work and liveliness. You have probably heard of the term "she is full of vim and vigor." This is a phrase reserved for those that will roll up their sleeves and go to work. Our job is to reach down and find

</td></tr></table>

a little extra energy, or at least stay away from being idle.

According to the Encarta Encyclopedia, "Sloths spend their entire existence hanging suspended from the boughs of trees. They move by advancing one limb at a time in a slow, deliberate fashion. Sloths descend only about once a week in order to relieve themselves. When placed on the ground they lie on their backs or crawl with the greatest difficulty.

"The sloth sleeps all day. An incrustation of a green algae forms in the hair of some species, making them indistinguishable from the surrounding foliage and moss.

"The animal is habitually silent but sometimes utters a low, plaintive call. It feeds chiefly on foliage and shoots, which are pulled within reach of the mouth with typical slow movements." (Source: Microsoft ® Encarta ® Reference Library 2005. Microsoft Corporation.)

Sloth can come about because we feel like moral weaklings, we claim we are powerless; we even begin to believe it. We say we can't change ourselves, let alone change the world, or live up to the standards we espouse. But virtue (like vice) has a level of depth. It isn't all or nothing.

So, we can slump toward sloth because we grow up and lose our youthful convictions; or because we feel like moral weaklings; or even because we get burned out. Maybe we become real social advocates, but then we might get frustrated that the world hasn't changed more due to our efforts.

And, so there comes a social and often a spiritual vacuum, and it has to be filled with something. We get bored, resentful, and lazy. Or we can feel suicidal. We begin to lose our humanity and start behaving like sloths.

We can have a remarkable ability to tune out what we do not want to hear. We can overlook the homeless in our own city, while exclaiming at the homeless elsewhere. We can believe what is convenient. We can blame "society" or an ethnic group or the government or our parents or our children or *anyone but ourselves* for our woes, because in most cases it comes to the choices that we—you and I make. Ours is the responsibility to *do something* about the problems we face, and to be a better citizen of our community, our country, our world.

Have you ever said or thought to yourself – *"I'm not responsible for the state of the world. I take no responsibility for things that are not my fault."* Sometimes I have even hinted that I am powerless to change things; or that I am too busy; or that the problems are too big, or all three. This kind of attitude will get us no-where fast, and nothing will ever get accomplished.

But I say there is something in you – that cares. I say there is something in you – that *wants* to leave the world a better place, and in a better state than it is.

Emily Schreiber decided at a young age that she could make difference in the fight for a cure for Cystic Fibrosis. Emily was diagnosed with CF at age nine. Although a surprise to her and her family, she confronted her condition with determination and resolve, putting together her first CF fund-raising event, dubbed *"Laps for CF"*, only six weeks after her diagnosis. An avid swimmer for years, Emily's idea for the fund-raiser focused on individuals pledging dollar amounts for each lap she would swim.

Emily's *Laps for CF* event has grown from swimming in a small community pool in Birmingham, AL to gaining the support of colleges and corporate sponsors. What began as a local swim-a-thon is now a successful CF non-profit organization with a variety of local and national events.

The most amazing aspect of *Laps for CF* lies in the story of its humble beginning, which is attributed to one truly remarkable young lady, Emily Schreiber.

Verse 17: *He that hath pity upon the poor lendeth unto the Lord; and that which he hath given will he pay again.*

Giving of our time, talents, and substance to the poor is a noble and worthy cause. It does not go unnoticed by God. In today's world of corporate profits that seem to permeate the airwaves and papers, it is comforting to know that there are those that will help others in need.

As I am involved with charitable work with Children's Miracle Network, and I see the corporations that we work with and how they become engaged in a charitable cause, I am pleased when they are willing to help children. There are many kinds of charitable causes that do good things, and there are many people who are willing to help others. I believe these good deeds do not go unseen by our Supreme Being. As this proverb points out, we have the opportunity to call upon the Lord when we may need His help someday.

Although it is a worthy cause to help those in need, we should not just show pity, but do something about it. Give to the poor; when a beggar asks you for money, take him and buy him lunch; when you have the opportunity to give to those in need do it; and if you feel like you are really passionate about a cause then spend some of your time building it and creating other avenues for fund raising.

It appears that between 300,000 and 500,000 Americans may be homeless on any given night. Most of these end up in shelters, and a good portion of those who don't are on the streets by choice. (According to *Newsweek*, New York City alone has 90,000 homeless, and 30,000 of these have AIDS or are HIV positive.) Most of these are adult men, but there are increasing numbers of women and children, and even entire families.

Demographic breakdowns of the homeless also vary widely from source to source. The following is an average of statistics found in several different sources, and is therefore only roughly accurate. It appears that about 15% of homelessness is due to job loss and lack of low-income housing. About 35% is due to mental illness, which is usually accompanied by marginal job skills. About 50% of the homeless are physically and mentally able, with job skills ranging from minimal to optimal, but choose not to work.

Many in the latter group are alcoholics or drug-addicts. They take advantage of public shelters and soup kitchens to save money for their addictions. Frequently they are the most cunning and aggressive panhandlers, while the willing-to-work are often too ashamed to ask for money, and not good at it when they do. The 15% whose adverse circumstances have put them on the streets are the subject of most of the media stories on street people. The sentiments this generates prompt further indiscriminate social services that often end up going to the wrong people, thus fueling the growing public cynicism about the poor that results in "throwing the baby out with the bathwater" (failing to help the truly poor because of resentment toward those who abuse the system).

When it comes to the poor and homeless, there are three primary questions. The morality question-"What is our responsibility to the poor?" The wisdom question – "how do we discern who the poor are and what they really need?" The practicality question – "what exactly should we do to help the poor?"

Your involvement, my involvement will depend on our willingness to give of our time and substance to help the poor. Corporations should be involved to help the poor and hold fund raising events to raise money.

The 100+ corporate sponsors that raise funds for Children's Miracle Network member hospitals I am involved with hold fund raising events, and they do so to help needy families receive medical care for their children. Roughly 8 million associates of these corporate sponsors participate in a variety of fund raising events. It is very rewarding to see others get involved and help the poor and needy.

Proverbs Chapter 20

Verse 11: *Even a child is known by his doings, whether his work be pure, and whether it be right.*

Have you ever thought of how others perceive you and your family name? To some this may not matter to them, to others the perception of what others think of them is one of the most important things in life.

We are known to others by the choices we make, and the actions we carry out. Our children carry our family name out to the world and they are known for their works. In business, our colleagues come to expect the way we will react to circumstances. So, the real question is what do others perceive us as? If we are perceived as someone they can count on how does that make our work experience become more rewarding?

Can we change the perception of others if it is not where we would like it to be? This could come as a result of our actions and we have a desire to change; it can also come as a result of others jealousy. I read a quote once that had a profound effect on me: *"When others speak evil of you, live so no one will believe them."* Sound advice.

Proverbs Chapter 21

Verse 13: *Whoso stoppeth his ears at the cry of the poor, he also shall cry himself, but shall not be heard.*

We have discussed this earlier, but it is interesting how Solomon comes back to the same wise counsel again to remind us to take care of the poor and needy. What is even more interesting is that this counsel is more stern and to the point: **if we don't listen and take some positive action for the poor, God will not listen to our cries when we need Him.**

When was the last time you did something nice for someone else? When was the last time you helped the poor; and did you help them learn something along the way that might help them get out of a bad situation? As a society, we need to do a better job and look into our own ranks and help those that we associate with.

Remember that we are all beggars and we call upon the Lord and each other in many instances to help us out, or to comfort us. Take heed that there are those right around you that are reaching out, even crying out for your attention. Will you turn them away…or will you extend a helping hand and bring a little joy into their lives? It doesn't take that long, nor does it require an enormous amount of effort.

When we are in the service of our fellow beings, we are serving God; and rest assured that our cries will be heard someday as well.

Proverbs Chapter 22

Verse 6: *Train up a child in the ways he should go: and when he is old he will not depart from it.*

My kids love to go into the mountains and spend time with the family. We wanted to provide fun, family experiences for our children that they could look forward to, and something that would give them lasting memories. Trips to the mountains seem to be the ticket: cheap; being in nature; many distractions or things to do; cool areas away from the heat of summer; and the list could go on and on. Ann and I love the mountains and the memories that the trips have created for us.

Taking family trips is one key aspect of training your children to enjoy nature.

My parents taught me to work and to not expect others to do things for me. *"Go out make something happen"* was the motto that my parents taught us. The same is true on religious matters. Mom and Dad taught the three of us to love God to keep His commandments, and to do good unto others. Today, I enjoy helping others, and I feel free and empowered by being obedient to what is right. This came from the example of my parents.

Proverbs Chapter 23

Verse 7: *For as he thinketh in his heart, so is he…*

First, I don't think anyone would argue that a positive attitude is what we need to be successful in life. But how far does a positive attitude take us down the path of success? Do our thoughts about who we are and how high we can reach really help in the overall day to day progress?

I believe self-confidence is a crucial gift that we need to possess. If our confidence is lacking we come across as weak and uncontrolled. When our confidence is at a peak we come off professional and poised in all situations. There are times when we can say that we are in a zone, and feel almost invincible. Wouldn't it be great to bottle these feelings up and open them up when we needed them…when our confidence may be lacking?

> **Key Point**
>
> If our confidence is lacking we come across as weak and uncontrolled. When our confidence is at a peak we come off professional and poised in all situations.

There are many ways to help us in this quest. But there are four basic elements to remaining self-confident:

1. Stop going down the destructive path of feeling insecure

2. Take note of your surroundings and look for things or people to help you

3. Don't boast about your abilities and accomplishments—let others do that for you

4. Ask God to bless you with wisdom and understanding

I thought it might be interesting to read what others have quoted about confidence. It can't be understated how vital confidence is for remaining at the top our game. A few quotes on remaining confident might help out:

> *"Don't wait until everything is just right. It will never be perfect. There will always be challenges, obstacles and less than perfect conditions. So what. Get started now. With each step you take, you will grow stronger and stronger, more and more skilled, more and more self-confident and more and more successful."*
>
> Mark Victor Hansen

> *"God helps those who help themselves."*
>
> Benjamin Franklin

> *"Too many people overvalue what they are not and undervalue what they are."*
>
> Malcolm S. Forbes

> *"Trust yourself. Create the kind of self that you will be happy to live with all your life. Make the most of yourself by fanning the tiny, inner sparks of possibility into flames of achievement."*
>
> Golda Meir

> *"Self Assurance is two-thirds of success."*
>
> Anonymous

Proverbs Chapter 24

Verse 1-2: *Be not thou envious against evil men, neither desire to be with them. For their heart studieth destruction, and their lips talk of mischief.*

This counsel is about as simple as it gets: stay away from evil and immoral people. They usually have two things on their mind: creating mischief and destruction. The primary thing to remember is that they only think of themselves, and what they want. They use others to accomplish their purpose, and then cast them aside.

Verse 17: *Rejoice not when thine enemy falleth, and let not thine heart be glad when he stumbleth.*

In business we must have a competitive element in our day to day affairs, in order to sell something, or deliver something to a customer. Sales creates revenue, and revenue generates profits, and profits pay for people and buildings, and advertising, and bonuses. I realize that we need to keep this cycle going in order to stay in business—that is not in question here.

What is in question is *how* we play the game and whether or not we boast in our own strength. Are we only playing to win at all costs no matter who gets hurt along the way? If so, we need to re-think how we are playing the game of business and ultimately the game of life. Look, I am an athlete that played four sports year round growing up, all the way through college. I was All-American in two sports, and All-State in all four sports. I set records, and played on state and national championship teams. The value of winning was and still is an important element in my life.

One of the important lessons that I learned during all those years of competing, is that someone will win, and someone will lose, but never to wish ill harm to anyone.

I remember a basketball game when it was a struggle for us to get ahead. We were the underdog, and we were getting clobbered in the second half. I got fouled pretty hard by their star player who was very cocky. The game went back and forth, fouls here, trash-talking there. At one point in the game, we came down on defense and their star player drove to the middle lane and took a shot, only to land on the foot of our center. The opposing player broke his ankle and I rejoiced! I justified that he deserved it, and that he got what he had coming to him. A player on the opposing team didn't like my rejoicing and told me to watch out. Of course I had to get in his face and do a little more trash-talking.

My Dad witnessed this incident, and after the game told me that he was very disappointed in me for expressing so much joy in the pain of another player. I tried to tell him that we were in the heat of battle, and that it helped us get an edge on the other team. Then he said something that was so simple, yet very profound. He said "That may be true that you got an upper hand on the other team, yet you still lost the game, and that young man that got hurt may not be able to play the rest of the season, which means he may not get a scholarship. Is that what you are happy about?"

Thanks for the wake up call Dad.

What kind of wake up call do we need to help ground us better in the things that really matter in life?

Verse 28: *Be not a witness against thy neighbor without cause, and deceive not with thy lips.*

This advice works in all walks of life. What is it about us humans that makes us want to bear false witness, or to deceive others with lies? Why are some people so bent on making themselves look good, and the other guy/gal to look the fool? It gets back to what we have discussed earlier, and it is plain and simple, *selfish pride.*

It comes down to two things:

1. We have done something that we will get in certain trouble for and if we pin it on someone else, we won't have to bear the embarrassment of looking stupid; and

2. We want to look better than someone else in the eyes of others, because this will help us to get the upper hand and the gain will be ours.

I have often been amused and disgusted at the same time, by the media and the politicians that have a never-ending stream of deceitful lies about someone, or something. They are able to spin the story into any direction they please. Reputations are scarred; feelings and names are dragged through the mud; friendships and other relationships are lost; secrets are sold to the highest bidder; and even wars are started due to the selfish nature of humans to get gain.

We as individuals and as a society need to stand up and make our voices heard when others are knowingly making false accusations.

Proverbs Chapter 25

Verse 9: *Debate thy cause with thy neighbor himself; and discover not a secret to another.*

Simply put, if you have a problem with your neighbor, family member, or business colleague go and talk to them directly and find a resolution. I have often stated that *Communication* is the foundation that builds solid relationships. When a breakdown in communication occurs, then other things begin to take shape and take over emotions.

We begin to think the worst is yet to come and we begin to protect our own interests when communication breaks down. So, before a relationship is lost; before a major conflict ensues; or before a war is started, go and sit down with the one you have a debate with and come to a resolution.

An approach to any type of conflict may take several steps to come to a resolution, but if you focus on even one, the end result will be beneficial to both you and the other party.

- Identify issues clearly and concisely

- Generate options (Brainstorm), while deferring Judgment

- Be open to "tangents" and other problem definitions

- Clarify criteria for decision-making

Take one issue at a time, starting with an issue that both of you agree is worthy of discussion. Try to make it a small bite, rather than the most difficult issue of conflict.

Generate several possible solutions to the problem, "brainstorming" ideas or otherwise making sure that all parties participate in the process. At this stage, it is important to defer judgments and evaluations of potential solutions, for to do so prematurely risks creating a "chilling effect" on the further generation of ideas. If one idea is rejected too quickly, other ideas may be similarly rejected without appropriate consideration. Even if you quickly identify an acceptable solution, it is useful to explore a few additional ideas before settling on the best answer to the problem.

Clarify the criteria that you are using for evaluating options. For example, one person may value a quick solution, while the other wants one that is longer lasting. One person may want to do something that is inexpensive, staying within current budgets, while the other person may feel that it is okay to spend more today to save money and stress in the future. As the leader, make a choice of how you will provide clarity and move forward.

Good solutions to problems emerge from mutually acceptable criteria being applied in a clear decision-making process. If it feels like the discussion has drifted into another area, check for clarification of the agenda at hand: "I'm confused. Earlier, we were discussing Issue A, now I hear you raising some concerns in a new area… is this where we want to focus, or should we return to Issue A?" This type of query can help clarify what the other person is intending, allowing you to either support this shift or express why you feel the original issue still needs your attention.

As you reach agreement regarding solutions to each of the problems being negotiated, *summarize these ideas in writing and restate them back to each other* to be sure everyone agrees with both the intent of the solution and its specific language.

If it is appropriate to leave things a bit ambiguous, until other issues are discussed, this is fine; just be sure that at the end of the discussion there is a clear record that accurately conveys to all parties - as well as others who may have a need to understand how the problem has been solved - what you are now intending to do and how you plan to do it.

In some cases a well thought out strategy is going to be more important that a well-written strategy.

Proverbs Chapter 26

Verse 11: *As a dog returneth to his vomit, so a fool returneth to his folly.*

I love this verse…it is amusing; true; and exceptionally disgusting all at the same time. We would never dream of throwing up and then eating it again (at least I hope not!), so why do people continue to do stupid things over and over?

Einstein once wrote that the true definition of insanity is *"doing the same thing over, and over again and expecting different results."*

If you are doing stupid things, stop. If you are engaged in more serious matters like addiction, please seek help from others who can offer you assistance and a helping hand—not money, a true helping hand.

> **Definition**
>
> **insanity** is *"doing the same thing over, and over again and expecting different results."*

If in business you have engaged in practices that you thought would bring in more sales, yet they do not over time, stop wasting your hard-earned money, and try something different.

The concept of returning to something unpleasant is not only dim-witted, it is a huge waste of time, money and other resources.

This reminds me of something I did in my early twenties that was silly and it still makes me laugh many years later. I was on a motorcycle riding trip with my new bride and some other friends. We encountered a sizable hill that had a pretty steep incline, with a hump right in the middle of it. It looked difficult, but for some reason, I felt compelled to conquer it.

I had a powerful dirt bike that I knew could get me over the top, and I could prove to the group that any hill was conquerable. The first trip up the hill proved unsuccessful as I hit the hump and flew threw the air on my way up the very steep face. I had to lay the bike down because I had landed sideways. Humiliated, I became more determined to be successful and climb the hill.

The second time up I hit the same hump, and a similar result occurred. Only that time I flew farther up the hill, but still unsuccessful. Now of course I was hearing the jeers of my buddies, and I determined to make it work.

The third time up was a disaster, and I flew over the top of the handle bars. You would think that that would have been enough to quit, but oh no, I now had something even more to prove. Up again, and again, and again. After the sixth time of crashing, my friends grew tired of watching me crash, and thought if they left I would just stop trying to impress them—before I got really hurt. They soon left the area and began riding around without us. My poor wife…she wanted me to quit before I got seriously injured, and she told me to stop. I'm sure my guardian angel had had about enough of my pride and stupidity as well! But, I was determined to be successful, yet 13 times up that stupid hill proved to be more than I could handle.

I never did climb the hill at that point, and my body was really hurting—not to mention my motorcycle was also taking a beating.

Looking back, I should have just moved to a different spot on the hill, and not tried to go up over the hump…*doing the same thing over and over, and expecting a different result.* Einstein was right. I felt like I was possessed and literally going crazy trying to achieve something that only needed some minor tweaking, like moving over 30 feet and going around that dreaded hump.

It was a good teaching moment, and thank goodness for a patient guardian angel!

Verse 27: *Whoso diggeth a pit shall fall therein: and he that rolleth a stone, it will return upon him.*

Quite an unpleasant thought to think that what bad experiences we purposely create for others may likewise be returned unto us. As humans we sometimes feel compelled to make things a little rougher for others, and look for ways to cause them to falter and stumble. Because of spite, or a bad experience we seek retribution for others actions against us either directly or indirectly. We go out of our way to place a stumbling block in the path of those that we want to get ahead of. "Digging a pit" for our neighbor, colleague, family member, foe, or whomever, has been a common practice in the human race for millennia…it is part of human nature.

Just because it is part of human nature, doesn't mean it is acceptable behavior. In fact it is childish and "so jr. high school". So again, why do people engage in this thought process?

This particular advice from Solomon states that if we plan on malicious impairment to come upon others, and if we purposely create a situation that causes harm to others, then it could very likely be brought back to us in return. Whether in this life or in the life to come, either way there is a reprisal that awaits us when we engage in such behavior.

What if we were to take a different approach and stop worrying about settling the score, or screwing up someone else's life? What if we were to take the higher road, and not pursue any type of destructive action upon others? It all sounds good in theory, but reality dictates otherwise…just listen to the 6:00 o'clock news, or read the headlines. Unfortunately the world is full of visceral hatred and spiteful intent to get even, or get ahead even at the cost of someone else's peril.

May I suggest that we train ourselves to act like an adult, and pass this along to our colleagues. But how do you go about training others to do the right thing and to help them to stop seeking some form of reprisal? We first need to start with ourselves and change our thinking. Then follow this simple pattern for helping others to take the higher road:

1. Help them recognize that what they are doing is juvenile

2. Suggest an alternative action--like communicating with the person

3. Encourage them to come to you (as a leader) and talk things through

4. Create an action plan for them to exercise good judgment

5. Follow up on their progress

Proverbs Chapter 27

Verse 2: *Let another man praise thee, and not thine own mouth; a stranger, and not thine own lips.*

Simply put, don't boast about your own abilities; let others do it for you. We have all seen celebrities, athletes, people that are talented in one area or another, that you just want punch in the nose, because it's always all about them. They are so cocky and so into how good they are. None of us like to hear others brag about themselves. It makes my stomach turn when I hear others brag about all the good things they have accomplished. I hate it even more when others trash talk about what they are going to do, then rub your face in their accomplishments.

So if we hate when others do it, why would someone enjoy hearing you or me boast about ourselves? Once again, the simple answer is: They won't.

Proverbs Chapter 28

Verse 19-20: *He that tilleth his land shall have plenty of bread: but he that followeth after vain persons shall have poverty enough. A faithful man shall abound with blessings: but he that maketh haste to be rich shall not be innocent.*

I love this verse. It tells us that rewards come from our hard work, persistence, innovation, planning and execution. It tells us that the get rich quick schemes are not out there, and to plan a meaningful strategy and execute on what you have planned. It reminds us that we should consider stopping and smelling the roses along the way and to enjoy the journey.

Far too often, we want to make a name for ourselves and acquire riches. In our haste to gather riches, we sometimes forget about enlisting the help of an almighty God that could open a few doors for us if it is an admirable endeavor.

Help may not always be granted right away, but a sincere ask can reap great rewards. Part of that "ask" is to have the fortitude and strength to carry on and be able to work through the challenges.

An Old Dutchman Teaches Us Work Ethic

Anonymous

Being from a well-to-do family didn't excuse me from work in the summer. A wise father, raised during the Great Depression, realized the benefits and discipline of hard work. He didn't want his son John to grow up soft.

When the boy was sixteen, he was sent to work with Pieter Van Heuvel, a sixty-something farmer. It was early June in central Wisconsin. Pieter contracted himself out to father to clear some land for him, for a golf course he was constructing.

It was a sweltering day when John reported to work in blue jeans, worker boots and a t-shirt. Pieter, dressed in dark green, bib overalls, seemed nonchalant about the sweat dripping from his forehead. He removed a greasy looking green baseball cap and wiped his forehead and flipped it back on his bald head.

He stood all of 5'4" in height and probably weighed 140 lbs. dripping wet. He emitted a knarly look. In a broken Dutch accent he said: "Ve vork hard, ve take 15 minute breaks twice a day, one at ten, one at tree. Ve eat lunch in thirty minutes. Din ve vork hard some more. Grab dat ax and follow me."

He did a whirlygig and before John could reach the ax, near a tree stump, Pieter was in the woods. John followed the thump, thumping sounds of chopping. When John reached him, he said: "Like deese." He grabbed a young sumac tree with his strong left hand and with one powerful blow, chopped it near the root with his right. He tossed the tree aside.

Then he moved to another and repeated the routine. And again and again. John probably stood there a half a minute, watching him in awe. He moved quickly, yet gracefully. He was wiry but muscular.

Suddenly he stopped and turned to gaze at John. "Vy you not vorking? VORK!" Immediately he re-turned to his chronic motion of chopping.

Two hours later, completely exhausted, John slumped to the ground. He remembered thinking: "thank God it's ten a.m." Pieter, sat on a log near me, sipping black, hot coffee from the metal cap to his Thermos.

He stared at John, then winked. "I thought you ver strong football player. You not in good shape at all. I'm old man, vy you not keep up vid me?" John didn't reply, just shook his head, wondering if he could make it until noon.

Well, he made it till noon and the end of the day. Pieter got him in shape and when John returned to school that fall, he was tough as nails. NO! Make that: as tough as Pieter. That was the most difficult and yet the greatest summer of John's life.

John learned from Pieter, not only the value of hard work in teaching responsibility, accountability and commitment, he also learned the good feeling of accomplishment and healthy self-esteem, that hard work delivers.

Key Point

Hard work teaches responsibility, accountability and commitment, and delivers the feeling of accomplishment and healthy self-esteem.

John remembered a line in the movie Platoon. One of the soldiers says: "after this, it's all gravy." That's how he felt after spending 90 sweltering days under the example of Pieter Van Heuvel. John is now 59 years old. "I've never been exposed to work as hard as that summer back in 1961," he said. "Since that day, everything was "gravy."

John thinks of Pieter often, if he were alive today, he'd be over 101. He could probably still be alive and chopping wood. What a man! And, what an example. John is grateful to two people for that summer job: Pieter for his tireless example of leadership and his father for having the **wisdom** to teach him one of his greatest life lessons.

Verse 27: *He that giveth unto the poor shall not lack: but he that hideth his eyes shall have many a curse.*

Taking care of the poor and needy is our responsibility. We are not to judge why they are in the circumstance they are, it is our obligation to extend a helping hand. I believe this is one of those literal guarantees, that what we sow, so shall we also reap.

Being charitable has so many benefits that it is difficult to count them all. The main point to bring up is that both parties win. Those that need the charity benefit from donations of time, money and other resources from others. Those that give the charity receive a good feeling that they were able to help, and they even get recognized as being a charitable person/organization.

Proverbs Chapter 29

Verse 2: *When the righteous are in authority, the people rejoice: but when the wicked beareth rule, the people mourn.*

The first two things that come to mind are: bad dictators and bad managers. I'm not real certain that I want to spend a lot of time here, but I do think it is important for us to realize that selfish, prideful, immoral dictators and managers cause the people they rule over to be unhappy souls.

Are you one of those managers? If you are, either step down, or make a change in your attitude. It really is as simple as that.

Why do the people rejoice when good leaders are in authority? I believe it comes down to how they use the authority given them. Is it for their own personal gain, or do they lead with the people in mind with the idea of how they can effect a positive win-win scenario? The key is to recognize what they promise, and what they deliver.

Verse 18: *Where there is no vision, the people perish: but he that keepeth the law, happy is he.*

When we endeavor to take on a task, or to lead others into a new venture, we must paint a picture of what the final result could look like if we apply knowledge, experience and hard work. It is much easier to follow someone who is passionate about achieving the end result, than it is following someone who is just going through the motions. So, when we talk of visionaries, we should have a brief discussion about what a *visionary* is, and why they are important.

According to Webster's Dictionary:

Main Entry: ¹**vi·sion·ary**

Pronunciation: \\'vi-zhə-ˌner-ē\\

Function: *adjective*

Date: 1648 **:** having or marked by foresight and imagination <a *visionary* leader> <a *visionary* invention>

I believe there are two crucial elements to being a visionary:

1. A visionary is one who can see the big picture; and

2. They are able to motivate others to move beyond their natural boundaries, and achieve something extraordinary.

Visionaries are leaders that tend to make others want to follow them. The world is filled today with visionary thinkers, people who have revolutionary ideas about reinventing our post-industrial society and embracing more innovative ideas on making something even better. Revolutionary thinking pushes the definition of status quo and challenges the current system to improve on what we have.

There are actually two parts to this discussion that are open for debate. The first, is the thinking that rather than simply "going along with the flow," a more inspirational goal is to "challenge conventional thinking," and do something good for mankind.

The first element "going along with the flow" is what many visionaries deemed to be boring and uninspiring. So, they along with others, decided to do something about it and think a little deeper, and come up with innovative ways to change how things were done.

On the flip side of the coin, history is full of people who "challenge conventional thinking," but failed to do something good for mankind. I won't waste the time or space on dictators, or immoral individuals who caused harm to humankind. Just know that the area to focus on is what they have done to help humankind, and how have they invented something, or some process that made our lives better?

Although Adolf Hitler challenged conventional thinking; but so what because he was pure evil and caused millions of innocent people to suffer and perish.

Who comes to mind when you think of visionaries? The list can be long and there are many over the past several millennia that deserve a brief notation for their contribution to society as a whole. Here are a few:

- George Washington

- Louis Pasteur

- Benjamin Franklin

- Steve Jobs

- Thomas Jefferson

- Your parents

- John Adams

- The entrepreneur

- Isaac Newton

- Vince Lombardi

- Abraham Lincoln

- Harry Truman

- Joan of Arc, or Jeanne d'Arc

- Genetics engineers

- Alexander Bell

- Michael Jordan

- Henry Ford

- Bill Cosby

- Susan B. Anthony

- Bob Hope

- John F. Kennedy

- Henry Aaron

- Martin Luther King

- Solomon

- Bill Gates

- Herb Kelleher

- Warren Buffet

- Fred Smith

- Billy Graham

- Gordon B. Hinckley

- Albert Einstein

- Oprah Winfrey

- Mother Teresa

- Sacajawea

"We cannot solve the problems that we have created with the same thinking that created them in the first place."

- Albert Einstein

So what do you and I need do to get on the list of visionaries? Well, we may not make the world's list of visionaries, but we can make that list with our family; our friends; and our associates.

When was the last time you sat down with your family or associates and talked through a challenge, or come up with a solution to a problem? If it has been a while then its time to re-examine your own talents and skills and come up with something good…even simple.

Proverbs Chapter 30

Verse 32: *If thou hast done foolishly in lifting up thyself, or if thou hast thought evil, lay thine hand upon thy mouth.*

You've gotta love the subtle, ancient way of telling someone to **just shut up and take a seat**. If you boast about yourself, or if you have done something stupid, put your hand on your mouth and walk away. It is actually kind of cool to hear an ancient wise man tell us all to take inventory of what we say, and to just shut up. I'm not sure it gets any better than that!

CHAPTER FIVE

Applying Wisdom in Business

"Never mistake knowledge for wisdom. One helps you make a living; the other helps you make a life."

– Sandra Carey

Now that you have acquired this wealth of knowledge on the topic of wisdom, what will you do with it? I would like to suggest that you use a little planning wisdom and map a strategy for improving how you think things through in more detail.

What is your filtering system to develop better skills and improve your life, as well as the lives of those you associate with? What kind of system do you presently follow to help you apply wisdom in business? If you don't have a system, let's put together some ideas on how you can acquire a procedure to always give you a solid path to follow.

We learn things in our work that becomes knowledge and experience. But I can honestly admit that many people that I have worked with over the years, have a lot of knowledge about a particular area, but they lack wisdom. They may have drive and ambition, but can't think through a problem or challenge in a logical fashion. How can someone be so brilliant in one area, and so out of touch in others?

We have touched on it earlier but I would like to offer a system for you to follow to help you stay on top of your game, and a way to assist you in coming up with solutions to common problems.

The six things I want you to focus on for this discussion are:

1. Listening

2. Vision

3. Clarity

4. Planning

5. Execution

6. Reporting

Since we humans like to think in three's, let's group the first three elements (Listening; Vision; Clarity) into one category called: *Leadership*

And the second group (Planning; Execution; Reporting) will be grouped together in a category called: *Strategy*

Leadership

Leaders are not created, but we can identify who they are. We need to do this early on and find those natural leaders that can make a positive impact on the organization. But even natural leaders need exposure to challenges and problems that arise. They need to be placed in situations that allow them to make decisions and follow through with solutions. They need the opportunity to take on challenges that hone their skills and generate the wisdom to reach their full potential.

Given proper motivation, individuals (and teams) will do their best—strengthening their organizations in the process of increasing their own effectiveness.

I believe all great leaders have these three elements constantly on the top of their minds: *Listening; Vision; Clarity.*

Good leaders, ones that others will follow into a burning building for the right cause, are those that take an in-

> **Key Point**
>
> Even natural leaders need exposure to challenges and problems that arise. They need to be placed in situations that allow them to make decisions and follow through with solutions.

terest in what others think, **and will listen** to others opinions. The answer, or solution may not always line up exactly with what the rank-and-file may have originally wanted, but because a leader took the time to listen, the majority of the people were given a fair shot at illustrating their thoughts and opinions prior to a solution being given.

We have most likely all read hundreds of stories of business leaders, politicians, children, and even parents that have not listened to their constituents and have done whatever they wanted to—in order to benefit themselves. These types of people in authoritative positions, (they are not leaders in my opinion) usually do not last long in positions of authority. The people rebel against the one in charge and no longer follow their counsel, or they may inadvertently become replaced if they choose to follow their own agenda all the time.

CEO's, head coaches, civic leaders, government officials are eventually replaced by the voice of the board or the people when they follow their own path for their own personal gain.

Think of it like a patient and doctor relationship. When a patient visits his/her doctor, they describe the problem, then the doctor asks questions about what the patient is experiencing. And, if the doctor does not listen to what is said by the ailing patient, and goes off trying to diagnose the ailment as one thing, then prescribes medication or rehab in the wrong the fashion, the results could be disastrous, even fatal.

So it is with how a leader must listen to his/her constituents. Leaders must **constantly listen** carefully to the problem in order to form a wise judgment and come up with the best solution possible.

Leaders must also **establish a clear vision** of where they feel the organization must be in the future. The next step

> ### Key Point
>
> Leaders must establish a clear vision of where they feel the organization must be in the future. The next step is to provide a vision of where your leadership can take the organization and what it will look like in 3 to 5 years.

is to provide a vision of where your leadership can take the organization and what it will look like in 3 to 5 years. What will be different, what will be better? ***Explain not only what it will look like, but how you will lead the team in getting there.***

Many leaders throughout the ages have identified what they want to achieve; laid out a plan of action; and executed a strategy of brilliant proportions. Solomon was one of those leaders who followed his plan to a tee as he built his empire. But think of others that have been instrumental in the devise of a strategy that clearly defined their vision and how they would achieve it.

We buy into a leader's plan more easily if it has been well thought out and articulated. Earlier we read: *Where there is no vision, the people perish:* the author (Solomon) decided to add in the phrase that the people perish when no one will step up and offer a vision of how to be successful.

The vision of loving parents is that their children will grow up and become productive contributors to society. Some parents start out by having an end goal in mind of what they would like their child to become, and what profession they would like to steer their child toward. They place things in their path such as education, friends, circumstances, etc. in order to affect the final outcome of getting them to adulthood and have their children take on a certain role in society.

Granted, it does not always work out exactly as planned, but there still was a goal that was initially conceived, and the vision of how to get there.

Thus it is the same in how an effective leader conceives what the future could look like, and the plans needed in order to get there.

Next the effective leader must **seek and provide clarity**. As a society we have not done a very good job at this. We don't seek clarity from others as often as we should, and it's probably because we don't provide enough clarity of what it is we would like to accomplish.

Think of the use of technology, particularly email, for just moment: it is a wonderful medium to converse with others and have a record of what was stated. But, it is a terrible way of communicating. ***Communicating a clear message takes dialog; sharing of ideas; push, pull, and an exchange of thoughts, ideas, opinions, body language and even feelings.*** The problem with email is that we can't see the body language used when the message was crafted. And to complicate this form of conversing even further, we use short, often terse sentences and think we have done a good job in explaining our ideas.

One simple way to test if our message has been properly understood is to ask for feedback from those who received our message. Ask them if the overall message is clear to them and what role they will play in order to achieve a successful outcome. Query the final result as they understand it and have them repeat what they will be contributing, and how they understand what your role will be in the process as well.

Providing clarity should become more of a responsibility of leaders, rather than a convenient way to achieve a goal. But remember that there are two sides to this equation: 1). seek, and 2). then provide clarity.

Strategy

Now, enter the area of strategy. I could write volumes about this topic, in fact I have! If you haven't done so already, read three of my books: Tactical Entrepreneur; The Complete Book of Business Plans; and The Business Game Plan. Two of these books have not only won several awards they are a simple, no-nonsense way of clearly understanding the processes of planning and developing a solid strategy. (Sorry for the selfish plug!).

The next element of our discussion in using *Wisdom in Business* brings in the concept of ***Strategy***, and includes **Planning; Execution; and Reporting.**

Proper Planning Presumes People Prevail Permanently. Oh come on, you've got to admit that was pretty clever! The point is that we stand a far better chance of being successful at just about everything we engage in if we plan out what we are doing prior to just jumping in.

I can think of many times in my life that when I was prepared, the better the presentation was, and ultimately the outcome was much better. I certainly don't mind flying by the seat of my pants once in a while, but when we are prepared, we come across more confident and sure of our message.

We should get into the habit of planning for the future and choosing our desired outcome. Can we actually plan for and achieve a certain outcome...yes we can! Why do you think business plans are an absolute requirement when seeking investment capital or new partners...? The potential investor wants to see how you have planned out the successful outcome of the venture that you are asking them to participate in.

They must buy into your plan in order to join you in your venture. Even when presenting to the board, executives must prepare a comprehensive overview with a well-thought-out plan and how it will be executed prior to any approvals are given.

<table>
<tr><td>

Profound Quote

"Great things are not done by impulse, but by a series of small things brought together."

-Vincent Van Gogh

</td></tr>
</table>

Vincent Van Gogh said: *"Great things are not done by impulse, but by a series of small things brought together."* What will yield greatness for you in business, or in life? Only you can decide this, but you can certainly make a good cause to affect the outcome. Here are a few ideas from others on the power of planning and how it can affect how you steer a positive outcome in your favor:

"If you are planning for a year, sow rice; if you are planning for a decade, plant trees; if you are planning for a lifetime, educate people"

— Chinese Proverb

"Planning is bringing the future into the present so that you can do something about it now"

— Alan Lakein

"Ruthless execution is the method and strategies that business leaders employ to break thought performance walls"

— Amir Hartman

"Let our advance worrying become advance thinking and planning"

— Winston Churchill

"Productivity is never an accident. It is always the result of a commitment to excellence, intelligent planning, and focused effort."

— Paul J. Meyer

"If anything is certain, it is that change is certain. The world we are planning for today will not exist in this form tomorrow."

— Philip Crosby

"If you employed study, thinking, and planning time daily, you could develop and use the power that can change the course of your destiny."

— W. Clement Stone quotes

Execution is up next, and it is as they say *"where the rubber meets the road."* We can talk a good game, and even plan until we are blue in the face, but at the end of the day, good execution will matter most. What results you plan for, and what you will achieve rests largely on how well you have planned the outcome. Now we have to put into motion what has been planned and anticipated.

During pre-game and post-game interviews, you will always hear of coaches and players refer to *execution* on the field of play. The training; the discipline; the studying; the practices; the mental preparation, and a myriad of things all comes down to how well a team, individual players and coaches can execute on the field.

So it is with business and in life. ***We must constantly remind ourselves that Execution is key to really achieving the pinnacle of success.***

Exccution is the realization of an application, or implementation of a plan, idea, model, process, design, specification, standard, or policy.

execution[2] `ex-e-cu-tion` *v.*

The act or manner of executing (actions, maneuvers, performances) or the state of being executed (accomplished.)
The battle plan was risky but its **execution** *was near perfect and thus ultimately succeeded.*

To become known as a successful strategist, a leader must also be able to execute the designs, processes and plans previously devised. If the execution breaks down the team stands a far greater chance of losing, or failing.

Case Study:

In 2006 Ford Motor Co. struggled to execute on reinventing the Ford Focus. The company executives allowed departments to clash with one another rather than looking for a way for departments to coordinate with one another. The company decided to update the Ford Focus but one problem existed: The North American operation wanted to simply refresh the existing model, while the European operation wanted to develop a new version of the model. The two groups couldn't come to an agreement, so they each traveled down their own paths and came up with their execution strategies.

The North American group updated the existing model and the European group developed a new model. As a result, Ford couldn't share parts or take advantage of economies of scale. There was a complete lack of coordination across the organization, and it cost the company millions in wasted time, parts, and separate operating plans.

> **Key Point**
>
> A complete lack of coordination across an organization can cost a company millions in wasted time, parts, and separate operating plans.

The Lesson:

Executing well is everything in business today. It doesn't matter how well designed your strategy is…how brilliant your vision is…how motivating your speeches are…if you can't bring it all to a successful execution.

Execution, of course, is the real bottom line, and what business managers must focus on as they seek to improve organizational performance.

On the other hand, a successful execution strategy must first have a vision that team members buy into. Then the leaders must be focused on achieving a flawless execution. In 2006 the Hewlett-Packard, CEO Mark Hurd was asked many times if he thought acquiring Compaq was a good idea. The question was irrelevant. Basically, Hurd said "What's done is done…", and his job was to find a way to make it work. He did just that when he reorganized the company into three divisions, with each division having its own sales force, making the heads of the divisions responsible for sales.

He also reorganized the IT function. Instead of having eighty-five data centers, he centralized them into three. What he did was decentralize the sales force and centralize the IT function of the company. This is the opposite of how the company was organized prior to the merger, and it proved to be highly successful. The new structure ensured the organizational structure would be better aligned with the business strategy. One measure of HP's success in 2006 was that operating profit increased by 31 percent.

Reporting is the next element of a sound strategy. The reason why reporting is so important is that it is more than just measuring how well we do.

Measuring performance is an excellent exercise to see how well we are doing. I talked a lot about Metrics in a previous book, ***The Business Game Plan.*** In it I discussed seven elements of a successful strategic plan. The sixth element reads: *A strategic plan will help you to establish metrics, or measurable results to apply against the success or failure of the plan.* It will also allow you to establish and achieve milestones along the way. In addition, you will be able to coordinate many new and important activities.

I once heard a quote that quickly summed up why it is so imperative that we not only measure our performance, but that we also report on progress.

> *"When performance is measured, performance improves. When performance is measured and reported the rate of improvement is accelerated."*
>
> - Thomas S. Monson

I love that…it is so simple, and yet very profound.

There is an important element of business that has to be considered when putting together your strategic plan—it is called measuring your accomplishments, or developing the proper metrics to help you measure what you are doing.

Metrics can be made up from a variety of business components. It all depends on what you need to measure. For example, you can be as specific as how many phone calls are made to the help desk that get resolved within a 72 hour period, or, as general as reaching sales goals in a given quarter. My experience has been that a good mix of metrics is often a desirable approach.

> **Definition**
>
> **met·ric**^{2} `me-trik` *n.*
> 1. A standard of measurement.
> 2. *Mathematics.* A geometric function that describes the distances between pairs of points in a space.
> 3. *adj.* Of or relating to distance

As your business needs continue to evolve and require new solutions that can meet your changing needs, management must continue to evolve to ensure that you have a team that employees and customers can trust and depend on. How will you measure your success? Since many enterprises are different, so too must the way in which an operation is determined to be a success or failure.

When you develop a set of *metrics* for your enterprise you provide a set of *blueprints* for all to follow. In the advent of metrics you should consider the importance of also developing reports that support your actions.

CHAPTER SIX

Imparting a Little Wisdom

*"I hope our wisdom will grow with our power,
and teach us, that the less we use our power the
greater it will be."*

-- Thomas Jefferson

The Founding Fathers of the United States of America studied the Wisdom of Solomon and the empires and trade that he established. Many leaders in the early days of the U.S. not only studied the success of Solomon, but followed his principles through the Freemason fraternity.

Some legends suggest that the society dates back to the time of Moses, but it is more probable that the beginning of Freemasonry dates to the construction of King Solomon's Temple in Jerusalem.

Today there are more than six million Masons worldwide, and when a man joins Freemasonry, *he learns of three great symbolic pillars:* ***Wisdom, Strength, and Beauty***.

So we have to delve into the question: *Why would these young patriots study an ancient King of Israel and try to learn from him?* The system that Solomon had built did not happen overnight, and the way he went about developing his kingdom was an interesting and educational study for the leaders of the young nation.

The Founding Fathers of the United States of America were influenced, and even inspired to create many great things and to form the foundation of a lasting society. This society needed to have all of the facets ingrained in the fabric of the entire system that would last for eons—despite the wicked intentions of conspiring men. This "king-dom" needed an eternally strong foundation that would withstand the onslaught of selfishness; greed; and conspiring hearts of wicked men who would want to turn the society into dictatorship.

In many cases the Founding Fathers would turn to the teachings of the ancient prophets and kings and learn of their ideas, intentions and actions. Many were students of Solomon and learned of his ways, and building practices. Indeed our discussion relating to the title of this chapter: ***Imparting a Little Wisdom***, is the wisdom that was pro-vided by many leaders during the past 3 millennia.

As we have previously discussed, Solomon's influence was widespread throughout the Middle East. His fame and fortune were derived from many years of careful planning and execution of his strategy. His allies were will-ing to come to his aid, and his people seemed to enjoy the wealth that he was creating for his nation.

The beauty of imparting a little wisdom to those who will listen is also genius in a small sense. Share some of the wisdom and the wealth, and allow others to experience a little suc-cess is what keeps organizations expanding and resilient with sharp people. ***Leaders that are willing to lift up others and let them taste of the good life with a little success, are leaders that keep and attract talented people.***

Solomon may not have even known 3,000 years ago that his wisdom would be the topic of many scholars, kings, prophets and av-erage "Joe's" as we all try to figure out what it truly means to be wise. Getting back to our earlier discussion of the definition of wisdom, Webster, Confucius, Buddha, and many other brilliant leaders have

Key Point

Solomon's influence was wide-spread throughout the Middle East. His fame and fortune were derived from many years of careful planning and execution of his strategy. His allies were willing to come to his aid, and his people seemed to enjoy the wealth that he was creating for his nation.

provided several in depth definitions to what Wisdom is truly all about.

Even Plato, weighed in on the subject of wisdom, said he,

> *"Wise men talk because they have something to*
> *say; fools, because they have to say something."*
>
> - Plato

Plato was a mathematician, writer of philosophical dialogues, and founder of the Academy in Athens, the first institution of higher learning in the western world. Plato is widely believed to have been a student of Solomon and Socrates and to have been deeply influenced by his teacher's unjust death. Non-the-less, he was wise in his teachings and was a great Greek Philosopher, and today we still quote Plato. Plato further uttered: *"Good actions give strength to ourselves and inspire good actions in others."*

All of this begs the question: Why were Plato, and Webster, and Confucius and Buddha, and the Founding Fathers, and yes, even Solomon so wise?

I believe it is because they were humble men who looked for inspiration to make a difference and help others along the way. Yes it is true that Solomon gained much wealth, he also asked a higher being, his God, to bless him with wisdom and understanding. Did he, along with the other wise men of their day, seek after higher learning, even hunger and thirst after learning? The answer is most likely yes, but they did so in an attempt to help others and to glorify God. In other words, their hearts were in the right place, and they sought to make a difference in the lives of the people they served.

Wise Souls of Our Day

Let's turn the clock forward a few thousand years from Solomon's time, and talk about those who impart a little wisdom today, in the past decade; in the past 50 years; even the past 100 years. Both men and women alike who seek to serve others and somehow make difference, seem to come from all walks of life. You can't just point to a society, or gender and say, *"oh yes, it is because of this or that they are so wise."* Men and women throughout the ages have been blessed with inspiration to know what to do and how to do it for the betterment of mankind. Their words have given solace and peace to millions throughout the ages, and have given thought provoking declarations for many to consider.

I would be remiss if I did not include my own parents in this discussion of Wise Souls of our Day. Jay and Marge Hazelgren, are the best parents in the world! I love them and honor them, and I'm so appreciative of their teachings throughout my life. They are humble people that work hard and love their family beyond measure. They have worked hard for my sisters, our families, and me and they are concerned about each every one of us…our successes, our failures… and everything in between.

What wisdom have they imparted? Let me begin with Simple Family Traditions. One family tradition that we have is to gather together for birthday parties. This is a way for the family to get together and enjoy each other's company, at the same time celebrate and have cake and ice cream! Who wouldn't want to gather together to have ice cream and cake?!

Another tradition to gather family together is a celebration of St. Patrick's Day. Although we are not Irish, my mother has a fun tradition of making everything green…including the food and drinks. Green bread, green jello, green punch, celery with green icing, and of course the traditional corn beef and cabbage meal. It continues with green plates, cups and utensils, green napkins, green table cloths, and yes we even wear little green hats to top it all off.

My Dad taught me to work. And, not only to work, but to enjoy what I was doing. Today my father is 77 years old and he still works 10 hours a day. He loves what he does and thoroughly enjoys staying busy working with landscaping and horticulture. The wisdom that he imparted to his children was to work for what you get, and what you want.

My Mother taught us how to respect others and to find the good in others. "Everyone has some good quality about them…just find it," she would say. Mom always wanted us to do good things and to help others. This endearing quality is how she has led her life, and to appreciate what you have. For Mom the golden rule is not just a nice saying in the Bible, it is a way of life. This is wisdom enough to help children get along and life and somehow look back to say they made a difference.

Key Point

I am forever grateful for loving parents who imparted a LOT of wisdom to my wife and me, and how they continue to inspire our children.

I am forever grateful for loving parents who imparted a LOT of wisdom to my wife and me, and how they continue to inspire our children.

My beautiful wife Ann is one of those wise souls that of our day that continues to keep me grounded in the ways of all that is good. My father in law, Gordon Christensen, once told that if I would just listen to her and come to a common ground, that I would never go wrong. He has been correct for many years.

What about other wise souls of the last 100 years that have done extra ordinary things? And, not just extra ordinary things, but they have exercised wisdom to build an empire; or they have influenced the lives of many others to make a difference in the human race. To name a few:

- Henry Ford

- Vince Lombardi

- Martin Luther King

- Warren Buffet

- Steve Jobs

- Bill Gates

- Mother Teresa

- Gordon B. Hinckley

- General Norman Schwarzkopf

- Lee Iacocca

- Robert Metcalfe

- Jack Welch

Women also strongly influence the U.S. economy. Women-owned businesses contribute $2.46 trillion and employ 19.1 million people, according to the U.S. Small Business Administration. The U.S. Census Bureau also reports that women control 80% of household spending. (Source: U. S. Small Business Administration, 2008)

Two points here: 1). There are many brilliant women in business spheres today that influence the way business gets done. Over the years I have worked with several gifted women and they are able to do more with certain areas of business that would otherwise be deemed a dismal failure if handled by their male counterparts. 2). When it comes to controlling the household spending in our home, my wife Ann is the absolute best choice to handle this task. I completely agree with both of these assessments by the U.S. Small Business Administration.

And, what about the most important inventions in the past 100 years? Many inventions have created new industries and have allowed organizations to build highly successful kingdoms in their own right. Some people would debate what the order of the top 100 inventions may be, but we should take a few minutes and at least list a few of them.

- Automobile/truck

- Oil exploration/Gas pumps

- Retail and grocery stores

- Cell phones

- Sports franchises

- Movies and entertainment

- Telephone

- Airplanes/jets

- Light bulbs

- Radio

- Television

- The Internet

- Personal computers

- The space program

- Email

- Computer Networking

- Inspiring Music

- Food processing

These and many other things are truly areas in our lives that have been influenced by the wisdom of others. We are the beneficiaries of so many industrious and wise choices of how others have spent their time and resources.

I often ask myself *"What are you doing with your time and talents to make a difference?"* I'm sure I am a little strange when it comes to this topic, but I feel it is an important that we need to ask ourselves often. There are many areas in our daily lives that we can do good things to make difference.

If you think about it for a minute, the things we say and do can a
big difference in the lives of others.
The time we spend doing extra ordinary
things, or even the little things can
bring joy and happiness to our family,
friends, acquaintances and countless
others that may learn about our actions.
Even a simple conversation can lift
someone's spirits at a time when they desperately need a few words
of good advice.

- What can your wisdom bring to others and help them in their
  life?

- You may not feel this is an important thing for you to ask
  yourself, but what if you can make a difference?

- What if someone is waiting for you to talk with them…or to
  send them a letter…or to invent the next innovative product
  that will rival the success of the personal computer?

Give it some thought, this is what true leaders do…they offer their
wisdom and provide additional insight to the complexities of life. In
the mean time…

Have you ever read something that really and truly speaks to you?
Have you read a quote, or a saying that appears to be written directly
for your benefit? I have, many times, and that is exactly why I wrote
this book in the first place: the Wisdom of Solomon was a true inspiration for me that I felt could help me to be a better person.

Solomon certainly isn't the only wise person that has lived on this
earth, and I have pointed out others that have given true inspiration.

For your enjoyment, here are a few quotes for you to ponder and
hopefully gain some additional insight:

Select Quotes on Wisdom

Give a man a fish, he'll eat for a day. Teach a man how to fish, he'll eat for a lifetime.

Ancient Proverb

God grant me the serenity to accept the things I cannot change, the courage to change the things I can, and the wisdom to know the difference.

Serenity Prayer

God helps them that help themselves.

Benjamin Franklin

Great beginnings are not as important as the way one finishes.

Dr. James Dobson

Wise men say nothing in dangerous times.

Aesop

Happiness is a butterfly, which, when pursued, is always just beyond your grasp, but which, if you will sit down quietly, may alight upon you.

Nathaniel Hawthorne

Happiness is not a reward - it is consequence. Suffering is not a punishment - it is a result.

Robert Green Ingersoll

He who knows others is learned; he who knows himself is wise.

Lao-Tze

Honesty is the first chapter of the book of wisdom.

Thomas Jefferson

I don't think much of a man who is not wiser today than he was yesterday.

Abraham Lincoln

"Beauty is truth, truth beauty" - that is all ye know on earth, and all ye need to know.

John Keats

A man dies daily, only to be reborn in the morning, bigger, better and wiser.

Emmett Fox

A prudent question is one-half of wisdom.

Francis Bacon

A road twice traveled is never as long.

Rosalie Graham

A single conversation across a table with a wise man is worth a month's study of books.

Chinese proverb

A single moment of understanding can flood a whole life with meaning.

Unknown Author

A smooth sea never made a skilled mariner.

English proverb

A wise man turns chance into good fortune.

Thomas Fuller

A wise person does at once, what a fool does at last. Both do the same thing; only at different times.

Baltasar Gracian

Man is honored for his wisdom, loved for his kindness.

S. Cohen

Maturity is achieved when a person postpones immediate pleasures for long-term values.

Joshua L. Liebman

Men are wise in proportion, not to their experience, but to their capacity for experience.

George Bernard Shaw

Much wisdom often goes with fewer words.

Sophocles

My experience has shown me that the people who are exceptionally good in business aren't so because of what they know but because of their insatiable need to know more.

Michael Gerber

Neither a wise man nor a brave man lies down on the tracks of history to wait for the train of the future to run over him.

Dwight D. Eisenhower

Never become so much of an expert that you stop gaining expertise. View life as a continuous learning experience.

Denis Waitley

Never leave that till to-morrow which you can do to-day.

Benjamin Franklin

Never mistake knowledge for wisdom. One helps you make a living; the other helps you make a life.

Sandara Carey

Nothing is a waste of time if you use the experience wisely.

Auguste Rodin

Be kind, for everyone you meet is fighting a harder battle.

Attitude: Quotes of Plato

Courage is knowing what not to fear.

Courage: Quotes of Plato

Good actions give strength to ourselves and inspire good actions in others.

Ability: Quotes of Plato

The beginning is the most important part of the work.

Beginning: Quotes of Plato

The most virtuous are those who content themselves with being virtuous without seeking to appear so.

Character: Quotes of Plato

We are twice armed if we fight with faith.

Belief: Quotes of Plato

Patience is the companion of wisdom.

St. Augustine

Knowledge comes, but wisdom lingers.

Alfred Lord Tennyson

CHAPTER SEVEN

Common Sense and Wisdom

"Common Sense is genius dressed in working clothes"
— Ralph Waldo Emerson

I was once asked what my thoughts were on the differences between *common sense* and *wisdom*, or if there really is a difference. This is a great question and deserves some discussion. I'd like to thank Paul Ditton for this intriguing question and for an opportunity to open up this discussion.

My answer to Paul's question basically came down to this: "Common sense seems to get lost far too often and is tossed out the window on a whim. Distinguishing wisdom from common sense I think requires three key ingredients: **1) good listening skills; 2) swallowing our selfish pride; and 3) exercising good judgment.**"

Once we are able to listen to a problem and think through some type of a reasonable solution, we are better off to come to a conclusion that allows others to take part in the benefit derived.

So is there a line to be drawn that makes up a distinct difference between wisdom and common sense? Does it really even matter if we are able to distinguish between the two? I believe the answer is yes to both of these questions, and I have put together a few opinions and discussion points that I hope are at least a little thought-provoking.

There have been times in my life that a total absence of common sense has existed and the world has taken a turn for the worse. I'm sure you have witnessed this at one time or another in your life and have realized the ugly truth that not everyone will always exercise common sense. Kind of sad-- but a true thing that exists today. Even the brightest, most talented people in the world seem to have a brain cramp once in a while and exercise poor judgment.

We shout about anything from our football team conceding three touchdown's in the last 10 minutes of a game; to the administrator who bans Christmas decorations because they are too dangerous; to the bank that won't give a father access to information about an account he holds jointly with his young daughter, for data protection reasons.

"Where was your common sense?" we say to our children when they have done something dim-witted even by their own standards. Or, even less common-sense oriented, we instruct them to use their common sense when we know they haven't got any.

Albert Einstein said: *"Common sense is the collection of prejudices acquired by age 18."* I am not sure that I agree entirely with this. On the other hand, it is true that sometimes what people claim as "common sense" is simply the refusal to acknowledge that there are complications that they do not understand, and that things are not quite as they seem at first.

Sometimes wisdom lies in maintaining simplicity. Sometimes, as Einstein would advocate, *wisdom lies in doing justice to life's complexities, and uncommon wisdom is required.* Einstein had it right. But though he understood the universe, the nuts and bolts of everyday common-sense life were not his concern.

Usually when I think of lacking common sense I have to turn to the Federal government. Of course, I could write volumes here as well, but won't. I will say however, that obtaining and keeping power seems to be the order of the day with most politicians, and when this attitude prevails, common sense takes a back seat.

The following is a funny satire of what could happen, even in heaven, when common sense takes a nap...will common sense prevail or will other regulations take over?

New arrival to St Peter: *I have led a blameless life these past eight decades.*

St Peter: *What has eight decades got to do with it?*

New arrival: *Well, it's a greater achievement to be good for eight decades than just two.*

St Peter*: That smacks of ageism to me.*

New arrival: *I was taught that age brought wisdom and is to be respected.*

St Peter: *Not under the new anti-ageism regulations. Neither old nor young get special consideration now.*

New arrival: *I am told I have been uncommonly good.*

St Peter: *Under the new regulations I am not allowed to discriminate on the basis of good behavior. It is considered that factors of race, sex and class might color my judgment.*

New arrival: *But it's common sense that a good man should have more chance of entrance to the Kingdom of Heaven than a bad man.*

St Peter: *The Kingdom of Heaven has been renamed to The Heaven Experience and we operate an equality of access policy.*

New arrival: *So be it, your sacredness, but may I in any case be admitted? I am old and have traveled far.*

St Peter: *You are doubtless a good man and a worthy candidate but unfortunately I cannot grant you entry.*

New arrival: *That makes no sense.*

St Peter: *Well, it's simply on health and safety grounds. Heaven is already full. Surveys have suggested that there is a one in a million chance that greater crowding will cause floods, fire or even total collapse."*

New arrival: *Common sense will tell you that I really deserve to be allowed in.*

St Peter: *Sorry, my son. I can't make any exceptions. It's more than my job's worth.*

According to an entry in Wikipedia, ***common sense*** *(or, when used to show a tribute as an adjective, commonsense, common-sense, or commonsensical), based on a strict construction of the term, is what people in common would agree: Some use the phrase to refer to beliefs or propositions that in their opinion they consider would in most people's experience be prudent and of sound judgment.*

It has often been said that the problem with ***common sense*** is that it is not that common. Instead most people make a choice in haste about a situation that deserves more thought and discussion. Age doesn't always matter when common sense should come into play; in fact, a lack of common sense would appear to be more prevalent in older people, commonly known as "people that should know better" than in younger people.

You don't need to know how things work as long as you know where to look for the answers.

One example of exercising common sense at a young age, is Jared Isaacman. Jared started at the age of 16 as a data entry specialist working in the IT department of a large credit card processing organization. After gaining experience in the back end working of the IT and credit card processing business, he set up his own company at the age of 17 and has

<table>
<tr><td>Key Point

You don't need to know how things work as long as you know where to look for the answers.</td></tr>
</table>

specialized in processing credit cards, and mergers and acquisitions. He set up his company from a simple premise that he could offer the same service at a cheaper cost, and provide a few extra incentives that other competitors did not offer.

In 2006, Jared's company was named number six on the Fortune 500 list, as they handled the merchant accounts for over 80,000 merchant locations. To run a hospital you don't have to be a brain surgeon. To run a furniture chain, you don't have to be a master craftsman. You just need to have a healthy dose of common sense, mixed in with a flare for a little risk, a little wisdom, and startup capital.

The primary argument is that common sense is not that common. If it was common everyone would have it and everyone would be able to make sound decisions. So, if it's not very common - then how do we gain it?

In business, and in every day life, one of the most important factors is to be able to make good decisions. But the biggest problem for any business is when the people in it are not running the business - instead they are running scared in case they make a decision and it turns out to be the wrong one.

One of the things I tell business owners, managers, my staff, my students and my children is never be afraid to make a decision. Of course, they will get some decisions wrong – we all do. But the person who never gets one wrong is the person who never makes a decision. The only thing I ask is to make sound decisions along the way based on solid data, or a good gut feeling, and see where it gets you.

If one of those decisions turns out to be wrong, then you need to identify it quickly. Deal with it if you can. Stop the bleeding, and move on.

And if you cannot deal with it, scream as loud as you can so colleagues can come to your aid. There is no shame in asking others to help you. That is what teamwork is all about, and that is a principle we all need to adhere to each and every day in business.

In today's business environment, to be a successful boss, you don't need always to know how something works. All you need is to know is where to look for the answers. The technological revolution, mainly through the growth and use of the Internet, has allowed us to access information very easily. Much of this book was researched using the Internet and finding various sources of information to form the basis of the discussions.

Common Sense is also vital when it comes to assessing the strength of your competition. No matter how good your organization feels it is doing; never underestimate the length to which other people will go to stop you in being successful. At some stage the competition could have the edge over you to such an extent that your business might go into reverse or even terminal decline.

You only have to look around where some of the biggest names - household names at one time -are no longer talked about as industry leaders. A prime example of this is IBM and personal computers. IBM is the company that first introduced the PC. It used to be a household name in the computer business. Today, IBM is only mentioned in areas of consulting, and not when it comes to purchasing a personal computer.

Sometimes, though, the ability to apply common sense in a big organization is difficult due to the nature of the tiered system of management. Case in point, strategy and communication sometimes get misinterpreted and lost en route to their rightful recipient. That is why it is even more important for managers to question what they are doing at all times.

For a small entrepreneurial business, which is usually operated by the owner, it is a lot easier to apply the common-sense principle without the obstacles of a corporate structure and all the inherent inefficiencies it brings with it.

If I were to ask you what common sense means to you, I think you might tell me that it means doing what is in the best interest of

__________________, and you would insert something like: the organization; the country; the family; the community, etc.

I am a student of U.S. History, and I love to learn about the wisdom of our Founding Fathers in forming a new nation and a Constitution that other countries still envy today. It is incredibly sobering and brings a swell of pride over me when I think of how they fought for the common good to be free to live their lives under a Republic, by the people and for the people. One of those patriots was Thomas Paine, who through his writings reminded the people and the politicians of his day, that common sense must always prevail for the growth and good of their new nation.

One important facet of learning about common sense, is to study the pamphlet written by Thomas Paine titled *Common Sense* in which he set forth arguments against British Rule of the newly formed colonies in America.

Born in Great Britain, Thomas Paine lived and worked there until his late thirties. He eventually migrated to the American colonies just in time to take part in the American Revolution. His main contribution was as the author of the powerful, widely read pamphlet, *Common Sense* (1776), advocating independence for the American Colonies from the Kingdom of Great Britain. In short, Thomas Paine's arguments against British rule consisted of the following elements:

- It was ridiculous for an island to rule a continent.

- America was not a "British nation"; it was composed of influences and peoples from all of Europe.

- Even if Britain was the "mother country" of America, that made her actions all the more horrendous, for no mother would harm her children so brutally.

- Being a part of Britain would drag America into unnecessary European wars, and keep it from the international commerce at which America excelled.

- The distance between the two nations made governing the colonies from England unwieldy. If some wrong were to be petitioned to Parliament, it would take a year before the colonies received a response.

- The New World was discovered shortly after the Reformation. The Puritans believed that God wanted to give them a safe haven from the persecution of British rule.

- Britain ruled the colonies for its own benefit, and did not consider the best interests of the colonists in governing them.

Less-quoted sections of the pamphlet include Paine's over-optimistic view of America's military potential at the time of the Revolution. For example, he spends several pages describing how colonial shipyards, by using the large amounts of lumber available in the country, could quickly create a navy that could rival the Royal Navy.

Take a moment and read some of Paine's quotes. They are not outlandish and do not promote some kind of hatred towards one man, or one race, or any religion. He simply states that America had an incredible opportunity before her to wipe the slate clean and begin again. He reminded the people then, and still reminds us today that America is the greatest nation on earth because of a Constitution and Declaration of Independence that ensures a system remains in place to promote freedom and liberty for all. And, that government never be in a position to dictate how freedom is earned, and how it is spent. Take a look…

Thomas Paine Quotations:

> *"…have every opportunity and every encouragement*
> *before us, to form the noblest purest constitution*
> *on the face of the earth. We have it in our power to*

begin the world over again. A situation, similar to the present, hath not happened since the days of Noah until now. The birthday of a new world is at hand, and a race of men, perhaps as numerous as all Europe contains, are to receive their portion of freedom from the event of a few months."

"There is something exceedingly ridiculous in the composition of monarchy; it first excludes a man from the means of information, yet empowers him to act in cases where the highest judgment is required."

"Some writers have so confounded society with government, as to leave little or no distinction between them; whereas they are not only different, but have different origins."

"I offer nothing more than simple facts, plain arguments, and common sense . . ."

"A long habit of not thinking a thing wrong, gives it a superficial appearance of being right, and raises at first a formidable outcry in defense of custom."

"Society is produced by our wants, and government by wickedness; the former promotes our happiness positively by uniting our affections, the latter negatively by restraining our vices. The one encourages intercourse, the other creates distinctions. The first is a patron, the last a punisher. Society in every state is a blessing, but government even in its best state is but a necessary evil."

"Time makes more converts than reason."

"Every thing that is right or natural pleads for separation. The blood of the slain, the weeping voice of nature cries, 'tis time to part'."

"But where says some is the king of America? I'll tell you friend, he reigns above, and doth not make havoc of mankind like the royal brute of Britain. ... so far as we approve of monarchy, that in America the law is king."

"That there are men in all countries who get their living by war, and by keeping up the quarrels of Nations, is as shocking as it is true; but when those who are concerned in the government of a country make it their study to sow discord, and cultivate prejudices among Nations, it becomes the more unpardonable."

"Wherefore, since nothing but blows will do, for God's sake, let us come to a final separation."

"Small islands not capable of protecting themselves are the proper objects for kingdoms to take under their care; but there is something very absurd in supposing a continent to be perpetually governed by an island."

I really like how Thomas Paine voiced his opinions, and that he chose to speak out and tell others about his beliefs about exercising common sense. He makes a good argument that supports the three points of difference in wisdom and common sense that we discussed at the beginning of this chapter.

The British Monarchy and the Parliament could not bare that uncommon peasants in America did not need nor want to be ruled by a King 3,500 miles away. Yet in contrast and in the humble opinion of the colonists, why would anyone want to be ruled by a monarchy that did not listen to common reason.

The Monarchy's pride became so overwhelming that the only thing left to do was to "whip those peasants into submission." Eventually good judgment would no longer prevail, and a long, expensive, and horrific war ensued.

Getting back to the three points of reference; they are not rocket science, nor do they finalize the argument that there is a distinct difference between common sense and wisdom.

They do however provide some additional insight into this important argument. Thanks to my new friends at the First Baptist Church in Salt Lake City, and especially for Paul Ditton, who posed this question to me in a fun discussion that we held on a snowy December morning.

So what have you learned so far about common sense and wisdom? I'm not going to review everything again, but I would like to point out that we all lack common sense to a degree, and when we do, it usually comes down to the three things listed at the beginning of this chapter:

Distinguishing wisdom from common sense requires three key ingredients:

1) good listening skills;

2) swallowing our selfish pride; and

3) exercising good judgment.

> **Key Point**
>
> Once we are able to listen to a problem and think through some type of a reasonable solution, we can come to a conclusion that allows others to take part in the benefit derived.

And again, once we are able to listen to a problem and think through some type of a reasonable solution, we can come to a conclusion that allows others to take part in the benefit derived.

Even Solomon with all of his wisdom, wealth, and wives (hey… www; the three w's; triple w; w^3) lacked common sense at times. When he began to marry outside of the covenant and began to erect small palaces for his wives to worship false idols, he became subject to commonality, and one who all of a sudden, *lacked* common sense. In short he offended the very God that had so richly blessed him for four decades.

So the question we need to pose to ourselves: *"Am I doing the*

*things in my life that warrant blessings...or chastisement from God?"
Is my wisdom in harmony with my common sense?* One way to test
this is to see where you are in your life. Are you receiving blessings
and do the heavens seem open to you? If not then maybe you need to
get back to the basics and show a little humility, and ask for help to
clarify what God wants you to do.

This test of course assumes that you have even the slimmest of
hope in a Higher Source, and that there could be a loving God that
will provide answers to you. I know that He will as long as you approach Him in a humble manner, believing that He can bless you, and
that you deserve the blessings.

Humility can open doors and will also give you confidence in the
presence of God. Every now and then we could all use a good dose of
humility without being forced to have more of it. We seem to be more
humble and open to suggestions from others, including God, when
things are not going quite as good as we would like them to. It is then
that we listen more carefully to direction offered by those we trust,
and again by a loving Heavenly Father who wants us to be successful.

My primary hope is to be humble enough to recognize His voice
in my personal and my business life, and to accept the things that
I can influence or change, and to have the strength to do His will.
Everything will eventually fall into place. These things are the basics
of Common Sense that Mr. Thomas Paine was trying to teach the
colonists of a newly formed nation.

CHAPTER EIGHT

SUMMARY

"A candle loses nothing by lighting another candle."
                                                    - Erin Majors

This journey for me has been a life-changing event as I have studied Solomon's Wisdom, and researched related topics. It has truly been a labor worth pursuing and I hope that some of my passion has come through on the pages.

We have a long way to go as a society to bring *wisdom and common sense* back into our daily business practices and even into our personal lives. But it is certainly not impossible to attain. We all have our part to play and make this life more meaningful for ourselves, our family; our community and our country.

The important questions are simple to ask, yet more involved to properly answer:

- What will you do with this information and ideas on increasing your own wisdom?

- Will you take the time to figure out how you stack up in the personal wisdom category, or just brush this off as something that is interesting?

- How will wisdom help you to become more successful in business?

- Does possessing true wisdom help you to become more prudent in your decisions?

- Do you consciously take the time to exercise common sense?

- Do you have a plan to increase your own wisdom, and when you do have a plan do you follow it?

I believe these are questions that we should ask ourselves periodically and figure out if we are gaining knowledge that actually helps us. Does this wisdom allow us to help others and make this world a better place? The answer is yes, and we all need to quicken our pace and gain as much wisdom in this life as we possibly can.

In review, the **12 Keys to Building a Successful Kingdom** are imperative to understand, and even more important to implement in the enterprise. If you think about it all 12 are important, and one key principle does not necessarily outweigh the others. Although if I had to vote for one, I would pay more attention to number 1, for when you seek after God's wisdom and align yourself with him, all other things fall into place.

12 Keys to Building a Successful Empire

I.   Seek Wisdom

II.   Provide Clarity

III.   Develop Strategic Alliances

IV.   Look for Opportunities

V.   Stay Focused

VI.   Purge Conflicts and Train Your Leaders

VII.   Hold others accountable

VIII.   Seek Prosperity and Expect to Win

IX.   Avoid Over Spending and Control Costs

X.   Exercise Integrity

XI.   Communicate

XII.   Exercise Common Sense

The book of Proverbs teaches us about human behavior and social organization, as well as spiritual values that can be used every day of our lives. We learned that the book of **Proverbs can be summarized under the following categories:**

- Seek True Wisdom

- Welcome Good Advice

- Steer Clear of Corrupt Friends

- Help Those in Need

- Avoid Improper Speech

- Enjoy Hard Work

On the order of **communication**, we could probably spend volumes here discussing the importance of communication in any organization. But as we learned earlier, a lack of communication or poor communication can lead to:

- Frustration

- Confusion

- Anger

- Mistrust

Better communication can have a positive impact on the organization and we must continuously strive to mount a defense to communicate in a manner that builds up the empire. Remember that **communication is the foundation that makes the enterprise function**. If the foundation crumbles due to poor communication, the rest of the structure follows suit, and the results are disastrous. Make certain that good communication always exists in the organization, and that transparency is at the top of the list.

An approach to any type of conflict may take several steps to come to a resolution, but if you focus on even one, the end result will be beneficial to both you and the other party.

- Identify Issues Clearly and Concisely

- Generate Options (Brainstorm), while deferring Judgment

- Be open to "tangents" and other problem definitions

- Clarify Criteria for Decision-Making

One important question that we need to ask ourselves is: *How do you and I build empires and processes in our day to day operations that will withstand the onslaught of destructive forces?*

Conventional wisdom would tell us to:

- create a blueprint;

- follow each and every step of the blueprint;

- develop a plan of action and follow the plan;

- update the plan when necessary;

- report our progress to stakeholders;

- execute the plan and make changes, or corrections when needed;

- review and assess where you are in the execution process;

- upon completion give credit where credit is due.

When you follow this type of wisdom, you stand a very high chance of being successful in just about anything you set out to do.

It is up to you and me to figure out the action plan and execute on a sustainable system.

Next, the system for you to follow to stay at top of your game, and a way to assist you in coming up with solutions to common problems comes down to six key areas.

The six areas we need to focus on for developing **true leadership and a solid strategy** are:

1. Listening

2. Vision

3. Clarity

4. Planning

5. Execution

6. Reporting

You can increase the likelihood that the message is received and interpreted as you intended by enhancing your communication skills using the following behavior.

- Take care to make messages non-offensive

- Try to communicate the message in a number of different ways - would a visual or an image enhance communications?

- Try to make connections between what the recipient of the message already knows and what are new concepts

- Look for clues as to the persons understanding - both verbal and non-verbal

- Make sure you check for understanding throughout the communication process

- Provide as much clarity as possible

Since most people like to think in three's, the first three elements (Listening; Vision; Clarity) can be grouped into one category called: *Leadership*. The second set of elements (Planning; Execution; Reporting) are grouped together in a category called: *Strategy.*

Next we studied the principle of **distinguishing wisdom from common sense**, and in order to achieve this it requires three primary ingredients from us:

1. Good listening skills;

2. Swallowing our selfish pride;

3. Exercising good judgment.

It has often been said that the problem with common sense is that it is not that common, probably a direct observation of a choice or decision being made that is overly complex and, ultimately, contrary to what would appears to be "common sense." I would submit that we all pay a conscious effort in keeping common sense on our minds, and ask ourselves if we are doing something for political or personal gain at the expense of exercising good old fashioned common sense. Stay the course, don't toss common sense out the window, and exercise solid judgment.

Learning is a journey that takes us through many facets of life. History has proven that there are certain individuals who have made a difference in their surroundings, and have gone on to help others in ways that can even be considered as brilliant. Solomon is one of those rare individuals who asked in a humble way to be a vessel for God and provide wisdom to his constituents, and then go on to be blessed immeasurably.

We each have the opportunity to bless the lives of others and ask for divine intervention to help us along the way. You and I can make a profound difference in the lives of others and reach out and lift them up in ways we have probably not even thought of. It all begins with a belief that we as human beings have something good to offer, and that there are people in need at our work, in our church, in our neighborhood, in our country, and yes, iJust to help drive home this thought of make a difference, I have included a few quotes on the topic that might be of interest to you. I hope you have enjoyed this book, and that you too will find out how you can make a difference if you choose to.

Never be afraid to do something new. Remember, amateurs built the ark; professionals built the titanic.

> \- Anonymous

Throughout the centuries there were men who took first steps, down new roads, armed with nothing but their own vision.

> \- Ayn Rand:

Two roads diverged in a wood, and I... I took the one less traveled by, and that has made all the difference.

> \- Robert Frost:

We must not, in trying to think about how we can make a big difference, ignore the small daily differences we can make which, over time, add up to big differences that we often cannot foresee.

> \- Marian Wright Edelman:

We must overcome the notion that we must be regular... it robs you of the chance to be extraordinary and leads you to the mediocre.

> \- Uta Hagen:

It's not the will to win, but the will to prepare to win that makes the difference.

> \- Paul "Bear" Bryant:

To put the world right in order, we must first put the nation in order; to put the nation in order, we must first put the family in order; to put the family in order, we must first cultivate our personal life; we must first set our hearts right.

> \- Confucius

Distinguishing wisdom from common sense requires three primary ingredients: good listening skills; swallowing our selfish pride; exercising good judgment.

- Brian Hazelgren

Someone is sitting in the shade today because someone planted a tree a long time ago.

- Warren Buffet

Can you really explain to a fish what it takes to walk on land? One day on land is worth a thousand years talking about it, and one day running a business has exactly the same kind of value.

- Warren Buffet

It is my hope that you have learned several new things as you have read this book. It is my further desire that you take this knowledge and make a difference in this world. Does Solomon's Wisdom transcend over 3,000 later? I believe the answer lies in how we interpret his sayings and how we apply those sayings and his wisdom in our life.

You have been given a gift to know that true wisdom can lead you to paths that you may have never known. Good luck on your journey to uncover uncommon wisdom and to apply its principles in ways that only you can make happen.

"There is one quality that one must possess to win, and that is definiteness of purpose, the knowledge of what one wants, and a burning desire to possess it."

Napoleon Hill

GLOSSARY

Buddha – Usually *Buddha* (or "the Enlightened One") refers to *Siddhartha Gautama*, the founder of Buddhism. He is usually referred to simply as "the Buddha", but also known as Siddhārtha Gautama (Sanskrit; Pali: Siddhattha Gotama). *Siddhārtha Gautama* was a spiritual teacher from ancient India and the founder of Buddhism. He is generally recognized by Buddhists as the Supreme Buddha (Sammāsambuddha) of our age. The time of his birth and death are uncertain: most early 20th-century historians date his lifetime from *circa* 563 BCE to 483 BCE.

Common sense – The practice of exercising good judgment without allowing selfish pride to make the decision for you.

Confucius – One was a Chinese thinker and social philosopher, whose teachings and philosophy have deeply influenced Chinese, Korean, Japanese, and Vietnamese thought and life. His philosophy emphasized personal and governmental morality, correctness of social relationships, justice and sincerity.

Frankincense and Myrrh – Symbols of royalty which were given as gifts in ancient times.

Free Enterprise Model – The formation of an idea into a recognized Opportunity that requires the development of Resources; Team; Strategy; Planning; Communication; and Assessment.

Free Masons – The modern history of the Masons begins in the middle ages with the stonemasons' guilds who built Europe's greatest cathedrals. Its membership includes more than stonemasons

– lawyers, businessmen, presidents, noblemen, and kings. Many of America's founding fathers were Free and Accepted Masons.

Today there are more than six million Masons worldwide. The public generally thinks of this organization in terms of a social fraternity like the Rotary Club, which is only partly correct. *Freemasonry* is a self-improvement organization, one of enrichment and of ideas where the member is ruled by intellectual capacity. A Mason dedicates and devotes his life to the Divine and eternal truth rather than to his own desires or any other worldly allegiance, which is perhaps why some of the most intellectually daring and creative people in history have been Masons.

Today when a man joins Freemasonry, he learns of three great symbolic pillars: *Wisdom, Strength, and Beauty.* Freemasons believe these virtues, represented by the Ionic, Doric, and Corinthian columns of ancient Greek architecture, are necessary for the creation, stability, and long life of communities. Since the 1700s, initiates have also been introduced to the tenets of Freemasons: brotherly love, relief, and truth. Freemasons strive to build upon the three pillars, sustained by the three tenets

The modern history of the Masons begins in the middle ages with the stonemasons' guilds who built Europe's greatest cathedrals. Its membership includes more than stonemasons – lawyers, businessmen, presidents, noblemen, and kings. Many of America's founding fathers were Free and Accepted Masons including George Washington, Paul Revere, Benjamin Franklin, and Thomas Jefferson. The list also includes Mozart, Goethe, Voltaire, and Haydn; Meriweather Lewis and William Clark; William F. 'Buffalo Bill' Cody, Tom Thumb, Irving Berlin, Louis Armstrong, and the Ringling Brothers; as well as John Wayne and Thurgood Marshall.

The earliest Masonic lodges existed in Britain in the early 17th century, but it was not until 1717 that four London lodges organized the Mother Grand Lodge of the World to govern themselves. The first lodge in America was set up in 1733 and was followed quickly by others, through which the Masons directly participated in the American Revolution and influenced the rise and spread of democracy.

The origins of Freemasonry relate directly to three communities: Judeo-Christian peoples, medieval stonemasons, and Enlightenment era thinkers. Though separate and distinct, these groups were united in their fascination with King Solomon's Temple. According to text in the Bible, wise King Solomon planned this Temple, and organized the stonemasons who built it. Its architecture and geometry were seen as perfect. Freemasonry's spirituality and virtues of wisdom and brotherly love came from Judeo-Christian beliefs. Freemasons modeled their organization and their ideal of relief from medieval stonemasons' guilds. Enlightenment intellectuals created the symbolic rituals that illustrated the concepts of beauty and truth for Freemasons. Based on these three traditions, the Most Ancient and Right Worshipful Fraternity of Accepted Free-Masons began in London in 1717.

While operative stonemasons use tools such as the level, compass, and square to fashion stone and construct buildings, speculative Freemasons use rituals and symbols to improve men and, through them, build better communities.

Floor cloths and charts used during the initiation of candidates are a good place to begin investigation of the material culture of American Freemasonry. Within the prescribed oblong indented border can be found the all-seeing eye, crescent moon, and seven stars. The black and white checkered floor representing the floor of King Solomon's Temple leads to one, two, or three steps representing various degree levels.

Set upon the mosaic pavement are the two architectural pillars of Jachin and Boaz surmounted by a blazing star with an open

Bible below. Stonemasons' working tools such as *the square, compass, plumb rule, level, chisel, mallet, and trowel* are distributed around the periphery, along with additional symbols representing specific degrees. Other symbols that are not considered tools appear in lodges as well. These include the beehive, Noah's Ark, and columns representing each of the five orders of architecture.

Hiram King of Tyre – Lebanese King that provided many building materials to Solomon for the building of the temple.

Holy of Holies – The Most Holy Place of Solomon's Temple containing two sculptured cherubim. It was separated from the Holy Place by a curtain.

Kingdom of Israel – Historians often refer to ancient Israel as the *Northern Kingdom* to differentiate it from the Southern Kingdom of Judah. The Hebrew Scriptures sometimes referred to the separate kingdom idiomatically as the "House of Joseph" in order to distinguish it principally from the "House of Judah."

Nathan – Known as "Nathan the Prophet." Appealed to King David with Bathsheba to have Solomon crowned as king. He later anointed Solomon as king of Israel.

Plato – a mathematician, writer of philosophical dialogues, and founder of the Academy in Athens, the first institution of higher learning in the western world. Plato is widely believed to have been a student of Solomon and Socrates and to have been deeply influenced by his teacher's unjust death. Non-the-less, he was wise in his teachings and was a great Greek Philosopher.

Queen of Sheba – Impressed by Solomon's wisdom and became an eventual ally of Israel.

Shimei – an enemy of King David and a threat to Solomon's throne. Eliminated by Solomon after he left the land of Jerusalem according to the pact he had made with Solomon.

Solomon – The 30th son of King David. King of Israel. Known to be the wisest of all men in the Eastern World. His wealth and wisdom exceeded all of the kings of the earth. The primary figure of *Everlasting Wisdom.*

The Ark of the Covenant – Contained the tablets of stone that God gave to Moses - The Ten Commandments.

Thomas Paine – His main contribution was as the author of the powerful, widely read pamphlet, Common Sense (1776), advocating independence for the American Colonies from the Kingdom of Great Britain, and of The American Crisis, supporting the Revolution.

Wisdom – accumulated philosophic or scientific learning-knowledge; Ability to discern inner qualities and relationships-insight; Good sense-judgment; A wise attitude, belief, or course of action.

Yemen – The Republic of Yemen or Yemen is a nation in the Middle East, composed of former North Yemen and South Yemen, in the south of the Arabian Peninsula. It borders Saudi Arabia and Oman on the north and the east. To the south is the Arabian Sea, and to the west is the Red Sea.

Index

Other products developed by Brian:

BOOKS

The Complete Book of Business Plans
Your First Business Plan
Tactical Entrepreneur
The Business Game Plan
The Entrepreneur's Game Plan

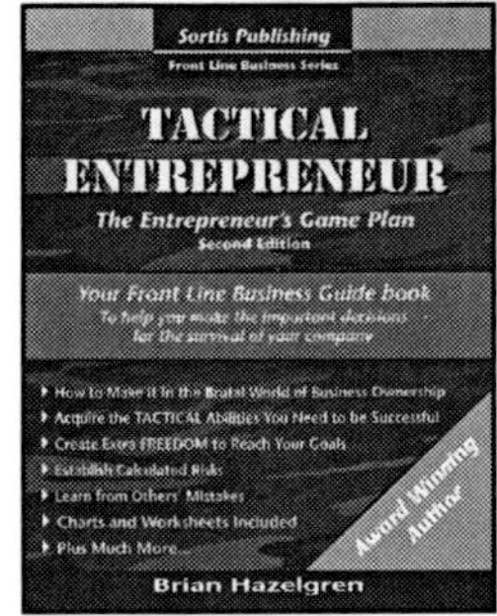

CD's

The Small Business Playbook CD Series

Visit **www.brianhazelgren.com** for more information

Brian is available for speaking engagements, key note addresses, corporate coaching, private workshops, and seminars.

He can be reached at:
brian@brianhazelgren.com

or by visiting:
www.brianhazelgren.com

LaVergne, TN USA
04 March 2010
174913LV00004B/19/P